Perfect 2

CROATIA

Travel with
**Insider
Tips**

MARCO ⊕ POLO

Contents

 TOP 10 4

That Croatia Feeling 6

For chapters: See inside front cover

TOP 10:

Not to be missed!
Our TOP 10 hits – from the absolute No. 1 to No. 10 –
help you plan your tour of the most important sights.

⭐1 DUBROVNIK ➤ 152
The 'Queen of the eastern Adriatic', with its *palazzi*, churches, museums and imposing defensive walls and fortresses, takes you back to that glorious era when it defiantly held Venice at arm's length.

⭐2 PLITVIČKA JEZERA ➤ 72
Tumbling waterfalls, turquoise-coloured lakes, luxuriant vegetation and dazzling travertine stone create a fairy tale-like landscape (left).

⭐3 SPLIT ➤ 120
The palace of the Roman Emperor Diocletian forms the heart of this bustling port. This is where Ancient Roman gods rub shoulders with Christian saints and trendy cafés with Roman remains.

⭐4 POREČ ➤ 96
Striking mosaics catch the eye in the Euphrasian Basilica, a unique ecclesiastical building from the early days of Christianity.

⭐5 TROGIR ➤ 125
This little port's historical splendour is omnipresent in the Old Town. The magnificent cathedral portal, with its countless figures, is a highlight of Early Gothic stonemasonry.

⭐6 NACIONALNI PARK KRKA ➤ 128
The Skradinski Buk waterfall is a popular attraction in this national park but there is much more to discover: secluded monasteries, shady walks and lush vegetation.

⭐7 HVAR ➤ 130
The international jet set congregates on the island of Hvar; the scent of lavendar and the romantic town of the same name attract the rich and the beautiful to Hvar.

⭐8 KORČULA ➤ 156
Aromatic white wines and unusual sword dances are the trademarks of this southern Dalmatian island. The attraction of the bewitchingly beautiful main town is its narrow alleyways, Venetian palaces and rustic taverns.

⭐9 PULA ➤ 98
Modern and ancient architecture in harmony. This bustling harbour town boasts a number of exquisite treasures from Antiquity – an amphitheatre, the Temple of Augustus and a triumphal arch.

⭐10 BRAČ ➤ 134
The sun, its beaches and the wind are the three plus points of this island that is one of just a few in Croatia that has a fine pebbly beach.

THAT
CROATIA

Experience the region's unique flair and what makes it so special – just as the Croats do themselves.

PROMENADING

See and been seen: no Zabrebian would want to miss their evening *korzo* on the **Trg Bana Jelačića** (▶ 48). There is a lot of flirting and cliques of teenagers giggling outside ice cream parlours. Young parents can be seen pushing prams and elderly men and women strolling along at their own pace. Everybody greets each other and catches up on the latest gossip. Just join the promenade and have a look for yourself – it's great fun (on summer evenings from 7pm onwards, in winter much earlier with many fewer people).

THAT BAROQUE FEELING

Varaždin (▶ 78) is Croatia's most beautiful Baroque town. When Croatian and international musicians **perform works from this era** in the Baroque halls and squares, some dressed in period costume, from mid September until mit October, you will find yourself transported back to the elegant 18th century with its lacy crinolines, smart uniforms and dainty dances (Varaždinske barokne večeri, mid Sept–mid Oct, www.vbv.hr).

MARKETS

As a contrast to all the sights of Ancient **Pula** (▶ 98), take a look in the elegant **Art Deco market hall** (Narodni trg, Mon–Sat daily until noon) where the locals really go to town bartering for a bargain. Here, a little unadulterated piece of everyday Croatia can be seen every morning. No Istrian would even conceive shopping in a supermarket when farmers bring their fresh fruit and vegetables to market every day. Not to forget the range of fish on offer either.

PEBBLES

Sandy beaches or ones with very small pebbles are rare on the Croatian coast. But the locals don't miss this at all. They love their bathing spots on the cliffs due to the crystal-clear water – and that can't be matched by any sandy beach. One particularly clean and picturesque **beach** with large pebbles is in the bay below the little village of Beli on **Cres island** (▶ 108). Don't forget your flip-flops!

FEELING

Pebbly beach in a lonely bay on the island of Brač

That Croatia Feeling

ON THE BALL

What do predominantly male inhabitants of **Split** (▶ 120) do on a late summer's afternoon? They head for **Bačvice beach** to the east of the town centre to play *picigin*. This variation of water polo, invented in Split, is played by up to five people in knee-deep water, doesn't seem to have any obvious rules and attracts an avid and critical audience. Why not join in?

GOING WITH THE WIND

No windsurfer should miss these hotspots: in the straits between **Orebić** on Pelješac and the little town of **Korčula** (▶ 156) the powerful *maestral* wind blows surfers along in a force six gale at 1pm on the dot. The only snag is that you have to watch out for ferreies and other people on the water in this narrow passage! And don't get carried away in your quest for speed either or else you will end up many nautical miles distant at the second surfing hotspot on the Dalmatian coast, the waters off Bol (▶ 135) on Brač.

SLADOLED – *GELATO* – ICE CREAM

A day without at least one tempting ice cream with a couple or more brightly-coloured scoops when on holiday on the Adriatic is virtually unthinkable! Simply the choice on offer and the juggling skills of the ice cream vendors are a delight themselves. The only question is: where is the best ice cream? The Ice Box in Poreč is a popular place but the champion could well be the Dolce Vita in Dubrovnik too.

WINE, MEN AND SONG

Croatian male-voice choirs call themselves *klapa*. And when they launch into their melancholic 'a cappella' songs, they will carry you away to a far off land of distant horizons and romantic sunsets with sailing ships heading out to sea and women waving to their departing lovers ... This traditional, heart-melting and contemplative music, often performed in simple pubs (*konobe*), is moving indeed and calls for a glass or two of wine afterwards as a form of emotional comfort – *živjeli!*

A break for an ice cream in Rovinj

The Magazine

1001 DALMATIANS
Island-hopping in the Adriatic

With more than a thousand islands to explore, the cleanest seas in the Mediterranean, no tides to worry about and a pleasantly mild climate, it is no wonder that yacht-owners love the Croatian coast. In the last deacde Croatia has emerged as a serious rival to Greece and Turkey as the Mediterranean's top sailing destination.

Over the past few years established destinations for passionate yacht-lovers, such as Hvar and Dubrovnik, have received a glossy make-over to compete as glamorous alternatives to the French Riviera where the café-culture rules and a fashionable bar scene swings in summer. Elsewhere, countless hidden coves – and some of Croatia's most secluded beaches – await those who can get afloat. And then there is the simple joy of having supper in a waterside *konoba* (tavern) and a *rakija digestif* before you return to your yacht moored in a moonlit harbour far from the tourist trail.

Island-hopping
There are three ways of island-hopping in the Adriatic. One is to use the excellent network of ferries, most of which are run by Jadrolinija (►38), that links the ports of Zadar, Split and Dubrovnik to the major inhabited islands. Another is to take a trip on a traditional *gulet* motorised sailing boat which usually spends a week cruising between the islands. Or, alternatively, you can take your own boat. You can charter yachts locally or make arrangements in advance (see panel opposite).

The basic choice is between a bareboat charter in which case at least one member of the crew must be an experienced sailor and a skippered boat, where you can help with the sailing, but pay extra for a captain in charge. Some operators also offer full-service yachts, complete with a captain, cook, steward and hostess. Another alternative is to join a flotilla – you have to be able to sail

FACTS AND FIGURES
- 1185 islands, of which about 66 are inhabited
- 5835km (3625mi) of coastline
- 4058km (2522 mi) of which are around the islands
- 60 marinas
- 350 natural harbours
- 13,000 berths

Boats moored in Dubrovnik harbour

your own boat but are part of a larger party where expert help is available if required.

In your own yacht you can choose where to stop, perhaps mooring one night in a trendy coastal town and the next in a deserted bay. Most of the 50 marinas are open all year round and all are within a day's sailing of one other. For a real back-to-nature experience head for the uninhabited islands of the Kornati archipelago near Zadar. Just beware of the *bora*, a strong northeasterly wind that blows from the mainland across the sea.

USEFUL WEBSITES

- Ferry routes and timetables: www.jadrolinija.hr
- Operators of 21 marinas: www.aci-club.hr
- Adriatic Yacht Charter: www.ayc.hr
- Yacht charter: www.clubadriatic.com
- Croatian tourist board, with full list of marinas and yacht charters: www.croatia.hr
- Bareboat and skippered charters: www.sailcroatia.net
- Flotilla holidays: www.sailingholidays.com
- UK tour operator with *gulet* cruises from Opatija, Split and Durbovnik: www.bosmeretravel.co.uk

The HOMELAND WAR

Just off the courtyard in Sponza Palace in Dubrovnik is a room in which the victims of the 1991–92 siege are commemorated. To most visitors, the photographs of dead teenagers, bombed buildings and the torn remnants of a Croatian flag from Mount Srdj provide a shocking reminder of the realities of war.

A young country

Stay in one of the buzzing coastal resorts in summer and you could be forgiven for forgetting the most important fact about Croatia – that this is a young country which emerged out of former Yugoslavia and is still recovering from the wars that tore it apart a little over twenty years ago. Head inland to Vukovar or the Serb villages around Knin and the scars of war are there for all to see in the burned-out houses and pock-marked façades. The emotional damage is less visible but it exists all the same. The few Croats and Serbs who remain in these areas share an uneasy peace, leading separate lives, drinking in separate bars and sending their children to separate schools.

Looking to the future

In many ways, Croatia is still in denial about what it calls the Homeland War. The first war memorial was inaugurated in 2006 in Zagreb's Mirogoj Cemetery, replacing a pile of bricks erected on a street corner by families of

Serbian soldiers shell Croatian targets, 9 February, 1993

the victims. Most politicians prefer to focus on the future, portraying Croatia as a modern, forward-looking European nation. But the world is not so easily convinced. Talks on becoming a member of the European Union were held up in 2005 over Croatia's inability or unwillingness to track down fugitive generals wanted by the international war crimes' tribunal in The Hague. Many soldiers accused of war crimes are still regarded as heroes in Croatia.

> 'Many of the soldiers accused of war crimes are still regarded as heroes in Croatia'

The end of an era

In hindsight, the wars of 1991–95 were an inevitable consequence of the break-up of Yugoslavia. The country had been held together by President Tito (1892–1980), a Croatian Communist fighter who came to power in 1945 after leading the Partisan resistance movement against both the Ustaše puppet regime of Croatia and the royalist Serbian Chetniks during World War II and was elected president in 1953. For 35 years, Tito managed to unite the various people of the Balkan states – Croats, Serbs, Slovenians, Macedonians, Bosnians, Albanians and others – behind his own brand of Socialism, rejecting both Western-style democracy and Soviet-style Communism and by combining the methods of dictatorship with a large element of personal freedom.

The Magazine

Ten years after Tito's death, Yugoslavia disintegrated. Croatia declared independence in 1991 and was attacked by units of the Yugoslav People's Army (JNA), a largely pro-Serb military force based in Belgrade. On the pretext of protecting the Serbian minority in Croatia, Yugoslav forces started to move into Serb-populated villages, establishing the Republic of the Serbian Krajina at Knin. Before long, the Serbs controlled a third of Croatia, cutting off road and rail links from Zagreb to Split and evicting Croats from their homes in a practice which came to be known as 'ethnic cleansing'. When Operation Storm ended the Serbian occupation in 1995, most Serbs fled to Bosnia. Although the war officially ended in 1995, parts of eastern Slavonia were not returned to Croatia until 1998.

> 'Croatia stands at the crossroads of cultures'

Croatia's war leader was Franjo Tuđman (1922–99), a former Yugoslav general who became a hard-line Croatian nationalist and the first president of independent Croatia. His successor, Stjepan Mesić, has instead adopted a much more liberal, pro-Western attitude, negotiating with the European Union and co-operating with the war crimes' tribunal. In 2005, he was elected to serve a second five-year term and, that October, handed over General Ante Gotovina, who had masterminded Operation Storm, to The Hague to stand trial for war crimes. However, a poll after the arrest found that 60 percent of the country considered Gotovina not guilty. The policies adopted by Mesić and his successors ultimately led to Croatia becoming the 28th member state of the European Union in 2013.

Balkan is a 'dirty word'

Most people have traditionally referred to the successor states of Yugoslavia as part of the Balkan peninsula, but these days 'Balkan' is considered a dirty word. Political leaders repeatedly call Croatia a Central European nation. In truth, Croatia stands at the crossroads of cultures. Torn for centuries between Venice and Istanbul and the Catholic

From left to right: President Tito, the memorial on the bank of the river Danube to those who died in war in the 1990s, war-damaged buildings in Vukovar

and Orthodox churches, it is no surprise that Croatia and Serbia were the catalysts for the worst war in Europe since 1945.

TIME LINE

c. 600BC
Greeks establish settlements on the Adriatic coast, followed later by the Romans.

7th century AD
Slav tribes of Serbs and Croats migrate to the Balkans.

925
Tomislav becomes first the Croatian king.

1094
The founding of Zagreb.

1102
Croatia becomes part of Hungary.

14th century
Rise of Venetian power in the Adriatic. Founding of the Republic of Ragusa centred on Dubrovnik. For the next few centuries, Croatia is fought over by Austro-Hungarian, Venetian and the Turkish-Ottoman empires.

1527–1918
Period of Habsburg (Austro-Hungarian) rule throughout most of Croatia, excluding Dalmatia.

1918
Croatia becomes part of the Kingdom of Serbs, Croats and Slovenes, later Yugoslavia.

1941–45
Nazi puppet government known as Ustaše assumes power in Croatia; Tito organises partisan resistance throughout Yugoslavia.

1945–80
Communist rule under Tito.

1990
Franjo Tuđman wins the first, multi-party elections in Croatia.

1991
Croatia declares independence. War breaks out with the sieges of Dubrovnik and Vukovar.

1995
Erdut agreement ends war with Serbia.

2005
Croatia starts negotiations with the EU. The Croatian general Ante Gotovina is arrested on allegations of war crimes.

2011
The parliamentary election is won by the Social Democrats: Zoran Milanović becomes Prime Minister.

2013
Croatia becomes a member of the European Union.

2014
After much deliberation, a high-ranking officer in the secret service suspected of murder is extradited.

NATURISM
THE NAKED TRUTH

As the tour boats enter the mouth of *Limski kanal* (Lim Channel), the passengers on board take out their cameras and binoculars to admire the view. Some of them get rather more than they were expecting, for this is the site of the biggest nudist colony in Europe.

The tradition of nude sunbathing in Croatia goes back a while. The first official nudist beach opened on Rab in 1934. Two years later, the British king Edward VIII and his lover Wallis Simpson asked permission to swim naked in Kandarola Bay. Croatia has had a laid-back attitude to nudity ever since.

Embracing the culture

While other countries tolerated nudism and confined it to out-of-the-way places, Croatia whole-heartedly embraced it, opening Europe's first commercial nudist resorts in the 1960s. Koversada, which began in 1961 on a small islet off Vrsar, has grown into a mega-resort, accommodating 7000 in campsites, bungalows and holiday flats. There are restaurants, shops and children's playgrounds, tennis, mini-golf and beach volleyball facilities and sailing boats for rent. This is merely the biggest of some 30 official nudist resorts, many of them in Istria.

You can dress as nature intended at hundreds of remote beaches and coves on the islands and along the Adriatic coast. As a general rule, the further you go off the beaten track, the more acceptable nudity becomes. Ask around at any busy harbour in summer and you will find boats willing to take you to nudist beaches on nearby islands. Even on popular family beaches, there is usually a section where nudity is tolerated.

In Croatia, the distinction between nudists and those who prefer to wear swimwear is gradually becoming less and less. Around ten percent of all visitors to Croatia sunbathe naked at some point and, for women, topless bathing is the norm. In the past, nudist beaches were strictly for nudists but these days 'clothing optional' is the rule. If you do visit a nudist beach and decide to keep your clothes on, just remember that staring is rude and photography is definitely out. Remember, if you take your clothes off – don't forget the sun-blocker.

What is naturism?

Naturism is defined by the International Naturist Federation as 'a way of living in harmony with nature, characterised by the practice of communal nudity'. It is not to be confused with sex or eroticism – as any visit to a nudist beach will quickly confirm. You can find more information on naturism in Croatia on the 'Croatia Naturally' website at www.cronatur.com.

Nudist beaches are quite common in Croatia

STAYING ON THE
FARM

Holidaying on a working farm is a relatively new form of tourism in Croatia. You can discover a lot about the traditional way of life led by the farming community in Croatia without having to do without creature comforts.

In the past, visitors to Croatia used to stay in one of the big package holiday hotels on the seafront, spending their days on the beach and their nights in the hotel bar, seeing very little of Croatia beyond their chosen resort. When tourism collapsed as a result of the 1991–95 war, the local people decided to take a fresh look at things. These days, the buzzword is *agroturizam*, 'agritourism', as more and more people return to their roots and open their houses to a new wave of visitors.

A breath of fresh air
Agritourism is breathing new life into rural Croatia. Old villages which were almost abandoned are being repopulated by a younger generation, eager to restore dilapidated stone farmhouses and develop organic agriculture. Driving through the inland regions you come across roadside signs

Lush countryside surrounds Motovun and the other hill towns of inland Istria

advertising *agroturizam, seoski turizam* or *seljački turizam*, which all mean much the same thing. It could be a stone cottage with a couple of spare rooms, or a grand farmhouse that has been turned into a luxury rural hotel, complete with a swimming pool in the grounds.

Leading the way

Istria is where agritourism has been most fully developed, helped by the local tourist authorities who have set up wine and olive oil routes and planned paths for cyclists and hikers. Tourist information offices have brought out brochures with a list of relevant addresses. There are now several travel agencies and websites specialising in tourism in the country and farm holidays, e.g.: www.istra.hr/en/about-istra/green-istria/country-side and www.findcroatia.com which provides useful links to other sites and lists of accommodation on (organic) farms.

With its olive groves, vineyards and Tuscan-style hill towns, Istria makes the perfect agritourism destination, especially as the sea is never far away. After an afternoon on the beach what could be better than to return to your cosy farmhouse for a delicious home-cooked meal of fresh local pro-duce, accompanied by the farmer's own wine and a welcome glass of herb brandy?

Agritourism is taking off

Other areas where agritourism is becoming popular include the Zagorje region, north of Zagreb, the villages around the Plitvice Lakes and the Baranja region of northeast Slavonia, near the Kopački Rit wetlands. You will also find examples of rural tourism on some of the larger islands such as Korčula and Hvar. Some places offer riding and have bicycles for rent,

A traditional wooden farmhouse in Lonjsko Polje National Park

The Magazine

others will let you join in with everything from feeding the animals to picking grapes and looking for wild mushrooms. Facilities vary, but what they all share is the chance for an insight into rural life.

Alternative accommodation

Those who really want to get away from it all can choose from some really unsual places to stay. How about holidaying in a lighthouse on the Adriatic coast, for example? Eleven such lighthouses have been converted into holiday apartments, sleeping between two and eight people. All have electricity or gas, hot and cold water, a TV and a kitchen, though you will have to take your own provisions for the week. Three of the lighthouses – at Makarska, Poreč and Savudrija – are on the mainland close to restaurants and shops. The one at Savudrija, on Istria's northern tip, is the oldest in Croatia, built in 1818. The others are all on islands, with varying degrees of isolation. The lighthouse at Palagruža, built in 1875, stands 90m (295ft) above the sea on the remotest island in the Adriatic, 70km (43mi) from Vis and halfway between the Croatian and Italian coasts. The island is 1,400m (4,590ft) long and 300m (985ft) wide, with its own beach and excellent fishing. Boat transfers can be arranged from Korčula or Split, but once there you are on your own. You can use your mobile phone to summon a boat or helicopter to the island in an emergency. There are two apartments each sleeping four and a resident lighthouse keeper for company. You just have to hope that everyone gets on well with one other!

Further infomation on staying in a Croatian lighthouse can be found at www.lighthouses-croatia.com. Accommodation can also be booked through this website.

A vineyard near Lumbarda on Korčula Island

BUILDING BLOCKS OF A NATION

Croatia's architectural diversity is a result of the vicissitudes of history that bestowed the country with new master builders.

Roman

The Romans conquered the Balkan coast in the 1st century BC, establishing the province of Dalmatia and building cities at Pula and Zadar. The emperor Diocletian was born in the Dalmatian town of Salona in 245AD and later built a palace for his retirement in Split.

Highlights
- The arena in Pula (➤ 98)
- The temple in Pula (➤ 99)
- Diocletian's Palace (➤ 120)

Byzantine

After the demise of the Roman Empire, Croatia was ruled from Constantinople and Orthodox Christianity became the main religion. The Slavic people who had arrived from the Ukraine converted to Christianity and built churches influenced by Greek and Roman architecture.

Highlights
- The mosaics in the Basilica of Euphrasius in Poreč (➤ 96)
- St Donat's Church in Zadar (➤ 137)
- The Church of the Holy Cross in Nin (➤ 137)

from top to bottom: The peristyle courtyard in Diocletian's Palace in Split, the Croatian National Theatre in Zagreb, the Gate of Hercules in Pula

The Magazine

Venetian

The finest buildings on the Dalmatian coast were constructed during the Venetian era between the 14th and 18th centuries. Master architects such as Juraj Dalmatinac (George the Dalmatian, c. 1400–73) and Nikola Firentinac (Nicholas of Florence) worked in the neo-Gothic style which marked the transition from the Late Gothic to the Renaissance. Sponza Palace and the Rector's Palace in Dubrovnik are both examples of this architecture. Most towns along the coast have Venetian-style loggias, usually adorned with the winged lion of St. Mark, the symbol of the City of Venice. In Dubrovnik, that separated from Venice in 1358 to establish the Republic of Ragusa, a search for signs of Venice's former sovereignty will be in vain although its architecture does bear many similarities to that of its major rival. Much of Dubrovnik was destroyed in an earthquake in 1667 and the harmonious townscape that can be seen today is in fact due to the fact that all of the Old Town was rebuilt at the same time.

Highlights
- Šibenik Cathedral (➤ 138)
- Trogir Cathedral (➤ 125)
- The arsenal and theatre in Hvar (➤ 131)

Baroque

The opulent Baroque style, characterised by ornate, brightly-coloured façades, was popular in northern Croatia during the 18th century as a symbol of Catholicism on the borders of the Ottoman Empire. The Baroque style reached its peak in the town of Varaždin that was briefly the capital of Croatia.

Highlights
- Varaždin town centre (➤ 78)
- The Tvrđa (citadel) in Osijek (➤ 85)
- Dvorac Eltz in Vukovar (➤ 86)

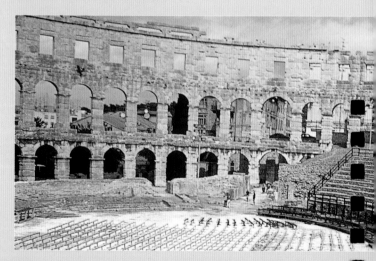

The 19th century

Grand public buildings combining elements of Classical, Gothic, Renaissance and Baroque styles were built towards the end of the Habsburg era.
The best examples can be seen in Zagreb's Donji Grad, the Lower Town.

Highlights

■ Trg Bana Jelačića, Zagreb (➤ 49)
■ Croatian National Theatre, Zagreb (➤ 66)
■ The seafront villas and promenade at Opatija (➤ 107)

Dubrovnik's walls

The restoration of Dubrovnik's town walls is one of the great success stories of modern Croatia. During the siege of 1991–92, they were repeatedly shelled and some of the citizens took refuge in the fortresses. Today, tourists once again stroll around the ramparts of this World Heritage town and there are few visible signs of damage. The walls as seen today date from the 15th century, at a time when the Republic of Ragusa felt under threat from the growing Ottoman Empire following the fall of Constantinople in 1453. The main towers were the work of Michelozzo Michelozzi (1396–1472), the chief architect to the Medici family of Florence; among others who worked on the walls was Juraj Dalmatinac, the architect of Šibenik cathedral. Up to 25m (82ft) high in places and supported by two free-standing fortresses outside the Pile and Ploče gates, the walls were not breached until Napoleon's troops entered the town in 1806. Ironically, the attack on the walls in 1991 first drew international attention to the war in Croatia. After the war, money poured in for their restoration.

The magnificent Roman amphitheatre in Pula is the sixth largest in the world. It was built in the reign of Emperor Augustus at the beginning of the Christian era and expanded under the Roman Emperor Vespasian (reigned 69–79 AD)

The Magazine

RIVER DEEP, MOUNTAIN HIGH
THE WILDS OF CROATIA

Mountains, lakes, rivers, waterfalls, forests, canyons and a sparkling blue sea – if you want spectacular natural scenery, Croatia has it all.

About 40 percent of the country is mountainous, with the rugged peaks and grey karst limestone of the Dinaric Alps providing a natural border to Bosnia and a dramatic backdrop to the Adriatic coast. The highest peak is Mount Dinara (1831m/6007ft) near Knin. Carved by gorges and riddled with underground rivers and caves, the Dinaric mountains actually extend further to the west under the sea,

left: Paklenica National Park is a popular destination for rock-climbing below: A meandering path through Plitvice National Park

above: Panoramic mountain view in
Paklenica National Park right:
The footpath around Zlanti Rat forest park
in Rovinj

their partially submerged summits
forming the Croatian islands.
Another 30 percent of Croatia is
covered in forests, primarily oak,
pine, fir, beech and spruce.

Croatia has always been passionate about preserving its natural
heritage. The first national park was
established in 1949 at the Plitvice
Lakes (➤ 72). There are now
eight national parks where wildlife
is protected and tourism carefully
monitored. A further ten nature
reserves include Kopački Rit
(➤ 80), the Lonjsko Polje (➤ 82)
flood plains and Mount Medvednica
(➤ 60) north of Zagreb. Nature
reserves offer a slightly lower level
of protection and access is generally
unrestricted, whereas a fee is
charged to enter the national parks.

Wildlife
As well as bears, other large mam-
mals that thrive in Croatia's mountains
and forests include the lynx, wolf

The Magazine

Croatia's national parks are also the home of golden eagles

and wild boar, all of which may be seen in the Plitvice Lakes, North
Velebit and Risnjak national parks. Red and roe deer are also common
and mouflon, a wild mountain sheep, are found on the Biokovo massif
beyond Makarska. Another common mammal is the pine marten,
a weasel-like mammal that feeds on small rodents and birds and has
even given its name *(kuna)* to the Croatian currency.

Birds of prey include golden eagles and peregrine falcons, particularly
in the Paklenica and North Velebit mountain ranges and a colony of
griffon vultures on the island of Cres. White and black storks nest in the
wetlands of northern Croatia in spring and summer, particularly in the
Lonjsko Polje, where you may also see egrets, herons and cormorants.

Dolphins frequently swim off the Adriatic coast and there is a school
of around 200 bottle-nosed dolphins around the islands of Cres and
Lošinj.

The great outdoors

Croatia is a paradise for walkers, mountaineers, cyclists, canoeists, sailors,
divers, extreme sports' enthusiasts and anyone who appreciates the great
outdoors. The tradition of mountaineering goes back a long way and
the highland regions have an
excellent network of well-
marked paths and mountain
huts. The lower slopes and forests are fine for gentle hiking,
but the higher mountains are
for serious climbers only. Even
in summer, when the coast is
bathed in sunshine, there can
be snow in the mountains.

NATIONAL PARKS
- Nacionalni Park Brijuni (▶ 103)
- Nacionalni Park Kornati (▶ 138)
- Nacionalni Park Krka (▶ 128)
- Nacionalni Park Mljet (▶ 159)
- Nacionalni Park Plitvička Jezera (▶ 72)
- Nacionalni Park Risnjak (▶ 107)

Croatia's national parks are a hiker's paradise

In winter, the mountain regions are bitterly cold, with sub-zero temperatures the norm. Anyone planning serious alpine walking should inform themsevles properly before setting out. For gentler walks, head for the Medvednica range north of Zagreb or the green hills of the Žumberak-Samoborsko Gorje.

Rock-climbers could try the challenging faces of the Paklenica and North Velebit national parks. Paklenica has more than 360 climbing routes, including a steep rock for beginners at the entrance to the gorge. Alpine and free climbing is also possible on Brač, Mljet and Vis and in the nature reserve Zlatni Rat at Rovinj. Canoeing, kayaking and white-water rafting are all popular activities, with various companies offering excursions on the rivers Kupa, Dobra, Zrmanja and Cetina. Rafting on the River Una, on the border between Bosnia and Croatia, can reach grades 4 and 5. The top rafting destination is Omiš, convenient for visitors to Makarska Rivijera or the Dalmatian islands.

> 'Croatia has always been passionate about preserving its natural heritage'

The bear facts

It is estimated that between 400 and 600 European brown bears live in the Gorski Kotar and Velebit mountain ranges, including the Plitvice Lakes and Risnjak national parks. The brown bear is the largest living land carnivore, weighing up to 300kg (660lb). Despite being virtually extinct in other parts of Europe, bears can be legally hunted in Croatia outside the national parks and it is more than disconcerting to find smoked bear meat and pâté on sale in smart restaurants and shops.

The Sword Dancers of KORČULA

The sword dance is a regular feature of life on the island of Korčula and has become a popular tourist spectacle.

The story begins with the *moreška*, a ritualised sword dance that arrived on the island of Korčula in the 16th century. Although its name derives from the Spanish or Italian word for 'Moorish', the roots of the dance have been lost in the mists of time. It is a variation of the mock battles between Muslim and Christian soldiers that were performed across the Mediterranean since the time of the Crusades. In Korčula, it was adapted to the local situation, at a time when the Venetian rulers of Dalmatia faced a constant threat from the Turkish-Ottoman Empire.

The story of the *moreška*

A familiar tale of good versus evil and, as always, good comes out on top. It opens with the Black King, dressed accordingly, dragging a pretty Muslim maiden in chains across the stage as he attempts to persuade her to return his unrequited love. The woman, Bula, had rejected him because of her love for Osman, the White King, who is confusingly dressed in red.

Good versus evil – the armies of the two kings come face to face

Magnificent costumes are a feature of the _moreška_

Eventually the two kings bring on their armies of followers, also dressed in black and red and the dance begins. To the accompaniment of a brass band, the two armies join battle, forming a circle as they act out the seven different movements of a highly stylised war dance, thrusting and clashing their swords in pairs. Each of the movements has its own rhythm; during the final movement, the sword clashes are fast and furious and sparks fly through the air as the Black King's army retreats into the

> 'The sword fighting is fast and furious and sparks fly through the air'

middle of an ever smaller circle before collapsing onto the ground and dying – defeated. The Black King surrenders his sword and the White King frees Bula from her chains with a kiss as the audience bursts into applause.

Moreška revival

By the end of World War II, the _moreška_ had almost died out and there were few people on Korčula who remembered the dance. It was revived by the local barber, school teacher, policeman and conductor of the town orchestra. These days, throughout July and August, a Festival of Sword Dances takes place across the island, with _moreška_ performances in Korčula town and the similar _kumpanija_ dance in Blato, Smokvica and Vela Luka.

On Monday and Thursday evenings in summer, the Sveta Cecilija dance troupe performs the _moreška_ on a special stage outside the Kopnena Vrata (Land Gate). And as thrilling as the spectacle may be, you will probably be thankful that the modern performance lasts 45 minutes instead of the traditional two hours.

CROATIA:
Tasty Delicacies Galore

There are many firm favourites in the Croatian cuisine – such as *čevapčići* minced meat rolls and pork *ražnjići* on a skewer, as well as the Croats' passion for charcoal-grilled steak. But Croatia has much more to offer and boasts a culinary variety that you would expect in a country where the Balkans meet Italy and central Europe meets the Mediterranean.

The menu in restaurants in coastal towns is strongly influenced by what is available locally. The classical Dalmatian cuisine focuses on plainly cooked fresh fish and seafood from the Adriatic that is either charcoal grilled or baked in a salty crust. Alternatives include *buzara*, a rich casserole of seafood prepared with tomato and white wine, or local bouillabaisse. The traditional main meat course is *pašticada*, beef stewed in a sweet wine or, on islands such as Pag or Creš in the Kavarner gulf where sheep farming is a mainstay, the spit-roast lamb is superb. The typical side dish is *blitve* made from chard and potates with garlic.

SIX OF THE BEST RESTAURANTS

In the past few years the nation's master-chefs have re-invented and refined several classical dishes. The following names should be on any self-respecting gourmand's list of places to visit:

- **Toklarija** (► 112): first-class Istrian slow-food in a rustically chic setting.
- Konoba Batelina (► 113): this restaurant near Pula is celebrated for its fish and its imaginatively presented dishes.
- **Zigante** (► 112): the flagship of a regional chain founded by the finder of the world's largest truffle.
- **Le Mandrač** (► 113): fusion food with an Asian touch served in a fully glazed dining room.
- **Zlatna Školjka** (► 145): sea bass on saffron rice is a typical dish served in this award-winning, slow-food restaurant on Hvar.
- **Kapetanova Kuča** (► 167): this harbour restaurant is famous for its oysters farmed in Mali Ston.

Classic Croatian fare: *čevapčići* and *ražnjići*

A truly Dalmatian dish is prepared under a *peka*, a metal lid covering a pot of food, on top of which charcoal is placed. Whether lamb, veal or octopus, this is slow food at its best, cooked with its tendons and fat to create a dish that is as succulent as it is flavoursome. Advance booking is often needed for a *peka* dish, but it's well worth it.

Delicious morsels

While the centuries under Venetian rule have enriched the Dalmatian menu with risottos and pasta, the Italian influence is most evident in Istria. This region in the northwest of the country – the best-kept secret destination in Europe for gourmands – boasts a cuisine that is as Italian as its dialect. Rustic bean-and-vegetable soup *manestra* or homemade *kobasice* (sausages), pasta such as *fuži* (fusilli) and *njoki* (gnocchi) can all be found. This is also the state which prides itself on prosciutto-style ham, *pršut* and especially white and black truffles *(tartufi)* which are rooted out around Motovun every autumn by crack man-and-dog teams.

Inland Croatia has more robust taste with a preference for produce from local farms. In the Zagorje region north of Zagreb, you'll find turkey (*purica*), endless varieties of cabbage and *štrukli*, miniature dumplings often filled with cottage cheese. Slavonia, like adjacent Hungary, prefers it spicy – paprika is sprinkled liberally on most dishes and gives *kulen* salami and the spicy *čobanac* stew their hot taste. A local speciality in the far east of Croatia is carp roasted on a stick.

FOOTBALL CRAZY

For a country with 4.3 million people, Croatia has enjoyed a remarkable sporting success on the international football stage with an impressive national team and enthusiastic fans.

After it was recognised by FIFA and UEFA in 1992, the team has made the grade for every major competition except Euro 2000 since its debut in Euro 1996 and finished third in the World Cup 1998 – no disgrace since it was beaten by the eventual winner, France, in the semi-final. In the World Cup in 2014, Croatia's national eleven was drawn to play in the same group as Brazil and knocked out in the preliminary round.

Regional pride goes to Dinamo Zagreb (www.nk-dinamo.hr) and Hajduk Split (www.hnkhajduk.hr). Fierce rivals, the clubs have monpolised the top spot every year since the formation of the Prva HNL league in 1992 and are the only Croatian league clubs to have played in Europe's Champions League tournament. Dinamo have the edge in silverware, with sixteen titles to Hajduk's six as of 2014.

A match at the 40,000-seater Maksimir stadium (▶ 66) in Zagreb or Split's 35,000-capacity Poljud stadium is a must for any football fan. Games are usually played at weekends in a home season that runs from mid-August to late-May. Tickets for games can be picked up at both stadiums, east and north of the town centres respectively, for as little as 30kn. International matches are usually played in Zagreb and advanced ticket purchases are a must.

A clash between Dinamo and Basel in Zagreb, during the UEFA Championship

Finding Your Feet

First Two Hours

Croatia is an easy destination to get to; bordering a number of European countries makes travelling by car and train relatively easy. Lying on the Adriatic coast also makes arriving by sea possible, however, the most popular choice of travel is by air to one of Croatia's many airports dotted around the country.

Arriving by air

Croatia's main international airport is at Zagreb, with regular flights on Croatia Airlines to all major European capitals. In summer, most visitors fly directly to one of the coastal airports at Dubrovnik, Split, Zadar, Rijeka and Pula.

Zagreb

- Zagreb airport is at **Pleso**, 17km (10.5mi) south of the city.
- **Facilities in the arrivals hall** include a bank, ATMs (cash machines), post office and diverse car-rental agencies.
- Croatia Airlines' **shuttle buses** run once or twice an hour to a terminal next to the bus station in Zagreb. The journey takes 30 minutes and tickets (30kn) can be bought on the bus. From the bus station, it is a 20-minute walk to central Zagreb. Tram no. 6 runs directly to the main square, Trg Bana Jelačića.
- A **taxi to central Zagreb** from outside the arrivals hall will cost around 200kn–250kn.

Dubrovnik

- Dubrovnik airport is at **Čilipi**, 20km (12mi) south of the town, near Cavtat.
- **Facilities in the arrivals hall** include a bank, ATMs (cash machines), post office and diverse car-rental agencies.
- Atlas **shuttle buses** drop passengers at the bus station and outside the Pile Gate for access to the Old Town. Note that return journeys to the airport do not stop at Pile Gate. The journey takes 30 minutes and tickets (35kn) can be bought on the bus.
- **Taxis cost** around 200–250kn to take you to the centre of Dubrovnik and 120kn to Cavtat.

Split

- Split airport is at **Kaštela**, 25km (15.5mi) west of the town near the Old Town of Trogir.
- **Facilities in the arrivals hall** include a bank, ATMs (cash machines), post office and diverse car-rental agencies.
- Croatia Airlines' **shuttle buses** drop passengers on the waterfront Riva. The journey takes 30 minutes and tickets (30kn) can be bought on the bus.
- A **taxi to central Split** costs around 250kn.

Airport Information

Zagreb: 060 320 320; www.zagreb-airport.hr
Dubrovnik: 020 773 100; www.airport-dubrovnik.hr
Split: 021 203 506; www.split-airport.hr
Zadar: 023 205 800; www.zadar-airport.hr
Rijeka: 051 841 222; www.rijeka-airport.hr
Pula: 052 530 105; www.airport-pula.hr

Arriving by land

■ The most direct but also the most over-crowded route across central Europe in peak season is via Salzburg (Austria), the Tauern Tunnel, Villach, the Karawanken Tunnel and on to Zagreb via Ljubljana. One alternative route from Villach is via Klagenfurt, the Loibl Pass and Ljubljana or else via Udine (Italy) and Triest to Rijeka. **Tolls** are levied on motorways in some transit countries.

■ If you are **travelling in your own car**, you will need a valid driving licence, insurance papers and registration documents. If you rent a car, confirm that your vehicle insurance is valid in Croatia before departure.

■ **Cities that can be reached by long-distance coach from a number of European countries** arrive at the main bus station in Zadar, Šibenik, Trogir, Split, Dubrovnik and Zagreb. Central Zagreb is a 20-minute walk or a short ride on tram no. 6.

■ **Train services from cities such as Venice, Munich, Vienna and Budapest,** for example, run to Zagreb. Central Zagreb is a 10-minute walk away or a short ride on tram no. 6 or 13.

Arriving by sea

Car and passenger ferries from Italy arrive at the ports of Zadar, Split and Dubrovnik. In summer, there are extra services to the more popular islands and also to Pula and Rovinj in Istria. All of these ports are within walking distance of the town centre, except Dubrovnik. From Gruž harbour in Dubrovnik, buses 1A and 1B run frequently to the main bus station and to Pile Gate.

Tourist Information Offices

There are tourist offices in all the main towns, cities and coastal resorts. Most staff speak good English and German and can supply you with free local maps and additional information. You will also find private tourist agencies operating in most towns and these are usually the best places to find private accommodation and book local excursions. The biggest private tourist agency is **Atlas** (www.atlas-croatia.com) which has offices all over the country. The head tourist information office is in Zagreb (tel: 012 415 611).

Zagreb
✉ Trg Bana Jelačića 11
☎ 014 814 051; www.zagreb-touristinfo.hr
🕐 Mon–Fri 8:30am–8pm, Sat 9am–6pm, Sun 10am–4pm

Dubrovnik, Pile
✉ Brsalje 5 ☎ 020 312 011
🕐 Mon–Sat 8am–7pm, Sun 9am–1pm

Dubrovnik, Gruž
✉ Obala Ivana Pavla II, 1
☎ 020 417 983
🕐 Mon–Fri 8am–3pm, Sat 8am–1pm, closed Sun.

Split
✉ Peristil
☎ 021 345 606, http://visitsplit.com

Pula
✉ Forum 3
☎ 052 219 197; www.pulainfo.hr

Opatija
✉ M.Tita 128
☎ 051 271 310; www.opatija-tourism.hr

Zadar
✉ Mihovila Klaića 1
☎ 023 316 166; www.tzzadar.hr

Makarska
✉ Kralja Tomislava 16
☎ 021 612 002; www.makarska-info.hr

Korčula
✉ Dr. Franje Tuđmana 4
☎ 020 715 701; www.visitkorcula.eu

Getting Around

Driving in Croatia

- If you travel to Croatia in you **own car,** you will need your driving licence, insurance certificate and registration documents.
- **Car rental** is available at airports and in all the main towns and resorts. You must be over 21 and have a passport, driving licence and credit card.
- The **best deals** are usually found in advance by booking online through one of the major international companies (➤below). If you need a car for a few days only, local companies offer competitive rates, though you should check carefully the levels of insurance cover and added extras.
- Keep your passport, driving licence and car rental documents **with you at all times** and never leave them in the car.

Insider Tip

Car rental agencies

Budget: 062 300 301,; www.budget.hr (Zagreb only)
Europcar: 098 231 089; www.europcar.com, offices in Zagreb, Dubrovnik, Pula, Rijeka, Split and Zadar
Hertz: 062 727 277; www.hertz.hr (Zagreb only)
Holiday Autos: www.holidayautos.com
Sixt: 016 651 599; www.sixt.hr, offices in Zagreb, Dubrovnik, Zadar, Pula and Krk

Driving essentials

- Drive on the right.
- **Seat belts** are compulsory for the driver and all passengers. **High visibility vests** (for all passengers and the driver!) must be on hand in the car.
- The use of **mobile phones** while driving is forbidden.
- **Headlights** must be on at all times in winter. A set of spare bulbs must be kept in the car (except for Xenon and LED lights).
- **Speed limits** are 50kph (30mph) in urban areas, 80kph (50mph) on minor roads, 110kph (70mph) on main roads and 130kph (80mph) on toll motorways. The maximum speed for vehicles towing caravans is 80kph (50mph).
- 0.5 ‰ is the limit imposed in the **drink-driving law,** for drivers under 25 years of age it is 0.0 ‰.
- In the case of an **accident**, you must call the police on 192.
- **Breakdown assistance** is available from Hrvatski Autoklub by calling 987.

Roads and tolls

- The 480 km (298mi)-long A1 motorway, from Zagreb to Metković, is going to be extended to Dubrovnik.
- The **A3 motorway** runs west from Zagreb to the Slovenian border and east to Lipovac on the border with Serbia.
- **Other motorways** connect Zagreb with Rijeka, Krapina and Goričan on the Hungarian border. There is also a Y-shaped network of motorways throughout Istria, linking Rijeka with Pazin, Pula and Slovenia and eventually joining up with the Italian motorway system.
- All motorways are **subject to tolls**. In most cases you collect a ticket at the point you join the motorway and pay on exit. Payment can be made in Croatian kuna, euros or by credit card. Typical toll fees for a standard car are 26kn from Zagreb to Varaždin and 174kn from Zagreb to Split.

- The most **scenic drive** in Croatia is the Magistrala highway which follows the coastline for 600km (372mi) from Rijeka to Dubrovnik. Although this is a spectacular drive, the road is single-carriageway for most of its length and gets clogged up with holiday traffic in summer.
- The distance from Zagreb to Split is 380km (236mi).
- **Tolls are also charged** for the Učka tunnel linking Rijeka to Istria, the Mirna bridge between Poreč and Novigrad and the road bridge to Krk.

Buses and trains

- **Buses connect main towns and cities** to outlying villages and coastal resorts. There are also regular bus services on the islands in the Adriatic as well as cross-country routes linking major towns for which air-conditioned coaches are used.
- **Bus fares from the mainland** to the islands, such as Dubrovnik to Korčula or Rijeka to Rab, usually include the cost of the ferry.
- For **timetables and bookings,** ask at the bus station or see www.autobusi.hr.
- The **railway network** covers most major cities, with the exception of Dubrovnik.
- **Most rail lines** are concentrated in the north and east of the country, making this an efficient way to get around inland Croatia but less useful on the coast.
- State-of-the-art express trains run between Zagreb and Split that cut the journey time to just a little more than six hours.
- **For timetables,** contact the main railway station in Zagreb (tel: 060 333 444) or see the Croatian Railways website (www.hzpp.hr).

City transport in Zagreb

- Zagreb has an **efficient network** of local buses and trams operated by ZET (www.zet.hr).
- The **main tram hubs** are the railway station, bus station and Trg Bana Jelačića.
- **Maps** are displayed at all tram stops.
- **Tickets** (10kn) can be bought from **ZET kiosks** near the terminals, in trams and buses and at news kiosks in Trg Bana Jelačića. At night, between midnight and 4am, a ticket costs 15 kn.
- **Tickets are validated** by slotting them in the punching machine behind the driver.
- There are heavy fines (150kn) for travelling without a ticket.
- If you are spending a few days in Zagreb, it is worth buying a **Zagreb Card**, valid for 24 hours (60kn) or 72 hours (90kn). It covers all forms of public transport, including the funicular to Gradec and the bus to Medvednica and give the holder a discount at museums.

City transport in Dubrovnik

- Buses in Dubrovnik are **operated by Libertas** (www.libertasdubrovnik.hr).
- The **most useful routes** are those connecting the hotels on the Lapad peninsula with the Old Town.
- Tickets (8kn) can be bought from **news kiosks and Libertas counters** outside the Pile Gate. They are slightly more expensive if bought from the drivers, who do not give change, so you should have the exact fare, 10kn.
- Tickets are **validated** by slotting them in the punching machine behind the driver.

Finding Your Feet

Taxis

- Taxis are available in **all main towns,** cities and resorts.
- **Fares are metered,** you usually pay a flat fare of around 30kn plus an extra amount per kilometre, with extra charges levied at night and on Sundays.

Ferries

- The **Jadrolinija ferry company** operates car and passenger services between the mainland and the major islands.
- There is also a **daily car ferry** from Rijeka to Dubrovnik in summer, calling at Zadar, Split, Stari Grad (Hvar), Korčula and Mljet.
- **A full list of routes, fares and timetables** is available from Jadrolinija offices and on the website (www.jadrolinija.hr).
- **Foot passengers** can simply arrive at the harbour and buy tickets from the quayside kiosk.
- **Car passengers** must join a queue which is often lengthy in summer, so at peak times it is best to arrive at least two hours before departure.
- **Reservations** are not possible on local ferries. Tickets and cabins for the **main Rijeka to Dubrovnik coastal route** can be booked in advance.
- Between June and September, there are **additional fast catamaran services** linking the islands to the mainland.

Jadrolinija offices
Dubrovnik: 020 418 000
Split: 021 338 333
Rijeka: 051 6 661 114

Accommodation

Croatia has a range of accommodation to suit all budgets and tastes, from large seaside hotels to rooms in private houses. In summer most hotel rooms are pre-booked by tour operators and package-tourists, but it is almost always possible to find private accommodation by asking around in local agencies or looking for signs advertising *sobe* (rooms) to rent. Some of the best examples of places to stay are listed at the end of the regional chapters.

Hotels

- The majority of hotels were built during the tourist boom between the 1960s and 1980s. Since then, most have been modernised and now have spa facilities and landscaped pool areas, etc. There is nothing in the furnishings and décor to remind one of the Socialist era any more when they were first built.
- **Most hotels on the coast and islands** operate from April to October, while hotels in Zagreb and inland are open all year. Book ahead during the peak months of June, July and August.
- A recent trend has been the opening of **small, family-run and boutique hotels** in the middle of historic towns. Many of these are members of the Association of Small and Family Hotels (tel: 021 317 880; www.omh.hr). Some of the best are listed at the end of the chapters on the different regions.

Private accommodation

- The **cheapest rooms on the islands and coast** are often in private houses. These range from comfortable apartments with a kitchen, bathroom and balcony, to a spare bedroom with shared bathroom in a family home.
- In **busy tourist towns**, you will be met at the bus station or ferry port by a gaggle of potential landladies offering rooms or holding up signs saying *sobe* (rooms) or *apartmani* (apartments).
- You can **reserve private rooms** through one of the travel agencies found in all larger towns and resorts. This will usually work out a little more expensive, but the accommodation is registered and of a guaranteed standard.
- There are **surcharges for tourist tax** and for stays of **less than three days**.

Agritourism

- One of the biggest growth areas has been in **rural farm stays** or agritourism (▶ 18) which has taken off particularly in Istria and inland areas such as the Zagorje.
- **Farm accommodation** is usually indicated by the signs *agroturizam* or *seoski turizam*.

Camping

- Croatia has **over 150 officially approved campsites,** equipped with hot water, showers and toilets. Many have restaurants and sports facilities, including swimming pools.
- The majority are **on the coast and the islands** while a few are inland next to rivers and lakes. Be aware that some of these campsites are **reserved for nudists.**
- Most campsites are **open from May to September.**
- **A full list of campsites** can be found under www.croatia.hr and www.camping.hr.

Off the beaten track

- A number of **lighthouses** have been converted into unusual self-catering accommodation (▶ 20).
- **Travel agencies in Murter** rent out old stone cottages on the Kornati islands for a 'Robinson Crusoe' experience. There is no electricity or running water and all the cooking is done by gas. Water comes from a well and supplies are delivered by boat twice a week. Contact Kornatturist (tel: 022 435 854; www.kornatturist.hr) or Lori (tel: 022 435 540; www.touristagency-lori.hr).

Driving through Bosnia

Check your insurance carefully if you plan to take a hire car into neighbouring countries, particularly Bosnia-Hercegovina, Serbia and Montenegro. An exception is often made for the area around Neum, a 9km (5.5-mile) corridor of Bosnia-Hercegovina on the Magistrala highway between Split and Dubrovnik.

Prices

for a double room per person and per night in the high season (in the low season prices are normally considerably cheaper):

£ less than 300kn   ££ 300–600kn   £££ more than 600kn

Food and Drink

Croatian cuisine is a fascinating blend of Mediterranean, Balkan and Central European influences. Regional cuisines reflect the country's history and geography, with light, fresh, Italian-style cooking dominating on the coast and heavier, spicier fare served in the inland and highland regions.

Eating out – a practical guide

- A *konoba* or *gostionica* is a **rustic-style tavern** specialising in more authentic Croatian cuisine.
- **Mealtimes are around** noon–3pm for lunch and 7pm–10pm for supper, though most places stay open throughout the day from 9am–11pm.
- Reservations are rarely necessary, except at the **smartest establishments.**
- Most places make a **small cover charge** for bread.
- It is customary to **leave a tip** of around 10 per cent.

What to eat

- **Starters** include *pršut* (cured ham) and *sir* (cheese).
- **Pasta dishes and risottos** are listed as 'warm starters', but are usually enough for a main course.
- **Fresh fish and seafood** predominate on the coast. Fish (*riba*) is usually plain grilled and sold by weight. Other popular dishes are seafood risotto, octopus salad, shrimp *buzara* (with garlic and white wine) and *brudet* (Dalmatian fish stew).
- **Dalmatian meat dishes** include *pastičada* (beef stewed with sweet wine), *janjetina* (spit-roast lamb) and veal or lamb cooked under a *peka* (metal bell) placed in the embers of a fire.
- **Istrian cooking** is heavily influenced by Italy, featuring *njoki* (gnocchi), *fuži* (pasta) and truffles.
- **Steaks and schnitzels** are popular everywhere, but especially in the inland regions. In Zagreb, look out for *zagrebački odrežak* (Cordon bleu).
- **Inland and mountain** cuisine is similar to that of central Europe, with dishes such as *gulaš* (goulash) and *grah* (bean stew).
- **Slavonian cooking** is particularly spicy, featuring *kulen* (salami) and *riblji paprikaš* (fish stew).
- The **national snack** is *čevapčići*, grilled meatballs served with raw onions, *ajvar* (spicy aubergine and pepper paste) and bread or chips.
- **Side dishes** include chips, boiled potatoes, rice, pasta, salads and *blitva*, which is similar to spinach and is either steamed or fried with potatoes, garlic and olive oil.
- *Pekarnica* (bakeries) sell a wide range of **bread,** as well as *burek* (filo pastry stuffed with minced meat or cheese).
- **Desserts** include *palačinke* (pancakes) with walnuts, chocolate or jam. A *slastičarnica* is a pastry-shop, most also sell delicious ice-cream.

What to drink

- Croatia produces an **excellent variety of wines.** Cheaper local wines are sold by the litre, whereas more expensive wines are sold by the bottle.
- **Red wines** to look out for include Dingač, Postup and Plavac Mali from the Pelješac peninsula and Teran from Istria.

Food and Drink

- **White wines** include Malvazija from Istria, Graševina from Slavonia, Grk and Pošip from Korčula and Vugava from Vis.
- Prošek is a **sweet red wine** from Dalmatia, an apéritif or dessert wine.
- **Mixed drinks** include *bevanda* (wine and water), *gemišt* (white wine spritzer), *bambus* (red wine and cola) and *miš-maš* (red wine and Fanta).
- The best brands of **lager** are Karlovačko and Ožujsko. Tomislav is a dark beer from Zagreb.
- Fierce **grappa-like spirits** are drunk both before and after the meal and are sometimes offered on the house by waiters. They include *šljivovica* (Slivovitz or plum brandy), *travarica* (herb brandy) and *biska* (mistletoe brandy from Istria). A sweeter alternative is *orahovac* (walnut liqueur).
- *Mineralna voda* (mineral water) can be either *gazirana* (sparkling) or *negazirana* (still).

Restaurant prices
for a meal with a starter, main course and a side-salad, without drinks:
£ under 120kn   ££ 120kn–250kn   £££ over 250kn

Shopping

The elegant shops and boutiques in the larger towns are much on a par with those in neighbouring Italy. The largest and most varied range of shops by far is to be found in Zagreb.

Practicalities

- Most shops are open Monday to Friday 8–8 and Saturday 9–2, although some **close in the middle of the day,** opening from around 9–1 and 5–8. In larger towns and coastal resorts in season, many stay open on Sundays.
- **Markets** are generally open Monday to Saturday from 8–2, though a few open on Sundays as well.
- The monthly **agricultural fairs** in the inland towns of Istria, such as Buzet, Motovun, Pazin and Vodnjan, have traditional local food, hand-made goods, folk music and dancing. Ask at the local tourist offices for further information.
- **Credit cards** are accepted in an increasing number of shops.

What to buy

- **Popular souvenirs** include lace from Pag, lavender products from Hvar, jewellery from Dubrovnik and gingerbread hearts from around Zagreb.
- **Artists sell their work** in the street at many coastal towns in summer. Some of the best places to buy contemporary art are Rovinj, Grožnjan, Dubrovnik and Hlebine.
- A **Croatian silk tie** (▶65) makes an unusual present.
- Croatian **wines, spirits, truffles and olive oil** all make good souvenirs. A wide selection can be found in local markets.

Entertainment

From top-class music and drama to traditional festivals, sports and outdoor activities, there is always something to do in Croatia. Details can be found from tourist information offices and in each of the regional chapters in this book.

Music and drama

- The top venue is the **Croatian National Theatre** in Zagreb (►66), home to the National Ballet and National Opera. Performances of more than 200 plays, ballet and opera are held here each year between September and July. There are also branches of the Croatian National Theatre in Osijek, Rijeka, Split and Varaždin.
- Almost every town along the coast holds a **cultural festival** in summer, with a series of open-air performances under the heading 'Musical Evenings' or 'Summer Nights'.
- The **big events** in Croatia are the summer festivals in Dubrovnik (►152) and Split (►120), with drama, opera and concerts in the streets of the Old Town.
- Another spectacular concert venue is the magnificent **Roman arena in Pula** (►98).

Folklore and festivals

- Croatia has a **rich folk music tradition,** from the *klapa* male voice choirs of Dalmatia to the *kolo* dances and *tamburica* (mandolin) music of Slavonia. Many hotels lay on folklore shows for their guests, but for something more authentic, try the International Folklore Festival in Zagreb in July or the folk festivals at Slavonski Brod and Đakovo (►90).
- The *moreška* **sword dance** (►28) can be seen on Korčula throughout the summer and at the Festival of Sword Dances in July and August.
- Most towns and villages have their own feast day, when the **patron saint's festival** is marked by a religious procession through the streets with fireworks and dancing.
- **Carnival** is also celebrated across the country, the biggest parades are in Rijeka, Samobor and Lastovo.

Sport and outdoor activities

- Croatians are passionate about **football** (►32) and there is huge rivalry between the two biggest teams, Dinamo Zagreb and Hajduk Split. The season lasts from August to May with a two-month winter break between December and February. Most matches are played at weekends and it is usually possible to get tickets.
- Croatia's **biggest tennis event** is the ATP Croatia Open, held at Umag in late July.
- **Swimming** is popular at beaches along the Adriatic coast. There are few sandy beaches. Many resorts have concrete sunbathing platforms with steps into the sea.
- Walking, cycling, climbing, horse riding, canoeing, kayaking and rafting are all possible in Croatia's mountains and rivers, **together with adventure sports** such as paragliding and canyoning.
- On the coast, numerous operators offer **scuba diving excursions,** while windsurfing is possible at Bol on Brač and Viganj on the Pelješac peninsula. Another option is to charter a yacht to explore the Kornati Islands (►135).

Zagreb

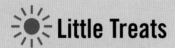 **Little Treats**

The taste of Croatia
Tasting is encouraged at **Dolac** market
(➤ 49) – but you should them at least buy
something too!

Mama mia!
The Croatian cuisine is celebrated in this restaurant run by the two sisters **Ivica and Marica**
(➤ 63): regional, seasonal, crisp and fresh.

Football crazy
Croatia's premier club **Dinamo Zagreb** (➤ 66)
is worshipped on its home ground. Go along
and see for yourself!

Zagreb

Getting your bearings

Zagreb, with around a million inhabitants, one in four of the country's population, is easily Croatia's biggest city. This is the political, economic and cultural heart of the nation, which makes it easy to forget that it has only been a state capital since 1991. For most of its history, Zagreb has lived in the shadow of Vienna, as a provincial outpost of the Austro-Hungarian empire, or of the former Yugoslav capital Belgrade. Only in the past few years has it rediscovered its confidence as a youthful, vibrant, forward-looking city.

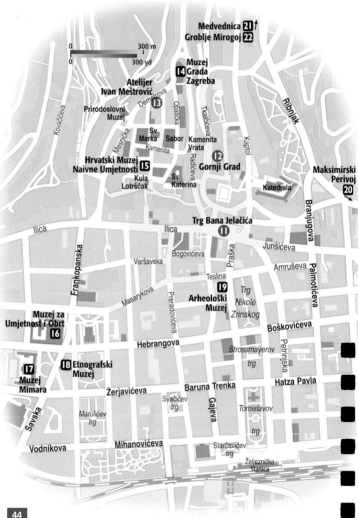

Getting Your Bearings

Zagreb lies between the wooded slopes of Medvednica to the north and the River Sava to the south. The Croatian metropolis originally consisted of two fortified hilltop settlements – the religious base of Kaptol, still dominated by its cathedral and the rival political capital of Gradec. Between them, these two make up the area known as Gornji Grad (Upper Town). In the 19th century, the city expanded and the Donji Grad (Lower Town) was developed, with wide boulevards, museums and grand Austro-Hungarian buildings linked by a green 'horseshoe' of parks, promenades and squares. Much of this district was built following an earthquake in 1880, giving the city a unified, central-European feel.

The two halves of the city meet at Trg Bana Jelačića, Zagreb's central square. With its popular outdoor cafés and hordes of commuters catching trams, the square is busy from morning to night and makes a natural starting point for any visit to the city.

The Croatian
flag flying
outside the
parliament
building

Two Perfect Days

If you're not quite sure where to begin your trip, this itinerary recommends a practical and enjoyable two-day tour of Zagreb, taking in some of the best places to see. For more information see the main entries (➤ 48).

Day 1

↑ 21 Medvednica
22 Groblje Mirogoj
14 Muzej Grada Zagreba
Atelijer **13**
Ivan Meštrović
Gornji Grad
Maksimirski Perivoj 20
Hrvatski Muzej **15**
Naivne Umjetnosti
12
Trg Bana Jelačića
11
Arheološki Muzej 19
Muzej za
Umjetnost i Obrt
16
17 18 Etnografski Muzej
Muzej
Mimara

Morning
Start with coffee and a breadroll on **11 Trg Bana Jelačića** (➤ 48), an essential Zagreb experience and the best place to feel the pulse of the city. While you're here, visit the tourist information office on the corner of the square to pick up a map and a Zagreb Card (➤ 50). After coffee, climb the steps to **Dolac** market (➤ 65), at its liveliest on weekday mornings.

Lunch
Take the funicular (left) up to **12 Gornji Grad** (➤ 51), arriving in time to see the cannon being fired from the Kula Lotrščak tower at noon. Have lunch beneath the tower at Pod Gričkim Topom (➤ 64) where wonderful views can be enjoyed from the terrace.

Afternoon
Take your time strolling around Gradec, with its churches, palaces and cobbled streets. There are several good museums here, but if you have time for only one, make it the **13 Atelijer Ivan Meštrović** (➤ 54), dedicated to the work of Croatia's greatest modern sculptor. Leave Gradec through the Kamenita Vrata (Stone Gate) and wander back down to Trg Bana Jelačića, pausing to visit the cathedral on the way.

Evening

The streets around Trg Bana Jelačića (opposite page, bottom) are at their best during the early evening *korzo*, when people dress up and promenade through the town. Stop for a beer or an ice-cream at one of the outdoor cafés on Bogovićeva before dining at the Restaurant Boban nearby (➤ 63).

Day 2

Morning

Time to explore Donji Grad (Lower Town). Begin outside the railway station by the equestrian statue of King Tomislav and follow a series squares laid out like parks northwards until you reach Trg Nikole Šubića Zrinskog (Zrinjevac), with its bandstand, fountain and statues. The **19 Arheološki Muzej** (➤ 59) is on one side of the square – after a quick look around, you can grab a drink at Lapidarium, a courtyard café surrounded by Roman sculpture.

Afternoon

Do what the locals do and escape from the city centre for a few hours. The easy option is to hop on tram 11 or 12 from Trg Bana Jelačića for a picnic in **20 Maksimirski Perivoj** (➤ 59). Alternatively, take bus no. 106 from outside the cathedral to **22 Groblje Mirogoj** (➤ 60), then walk down the hill and pick up the tram to **21 Medvednica** (➤ 60). Check with the tourist office whether the cable car is running, or else buses from Mihaljevac will whisk you up the mountain, if you have the energy, walk back through the woods before returning to Trg Bana Jelačića by tram.

Evening

Ask at the tourist office for a copy of their monthly leaflet of concert and theatre listings. If you can, take in a show at the Hrvatsko Narodno Kazalište (Croatian National Theatre, above), a sumptuous opera house which opened in 1895 (➤ 66).

⏱ Trg Bana Jelačića

This broad, paved square, where the Old Town meets the new, is the symbolic heart of Zagreb. Café life rules here, with everyone from the president downwards meeting at the outdoor cafés on weekend mornings to read the newspapers, talk politics, sport and gossip. Cars are not allowed in the square, but trams trundle to and fro, bringing commuters and shoppers from the outlying suburbs. With newspaper kiosks and flower stalls against a backdrop of imposing 19th-century Habsburg architecture, Trg Bana Jelačića central square presents a lively scene.

It was laid out as the city's main square in 1850, but its present character dates from 1866, when the **equestrian statue** of Governor Josip Jelačić (1801–59) was placed here, seven years after his death. This popular figure was appointed to quell anti-Hungarian feeling and the statue recalls his triumphant entry into Zagreb in 1848. Despite being a servant of the Austro-Hungarian empire, he became an ardent Croatian nationalist, he abolished feudalism, waged war on Hungary and united Croatia, Slavonia and Dalmatia into a single state.

The statue has witnessed changing fortunes over the years. In 1947, after the Communists took power, it was dismantled and replaced with a monument to socialist women, while the square was renamed Trg Republike (Republic Square). The statue was never destroyed, but kept in a cellar by a museum curator, ready for its eventual restoration. Finally, in 1990, as Croatia prepared for independence, this symbol of Croatian nationalism was returned to its original setting, only this time the governor's sword pointed not to the old enemy in Budapest but to the new one in Belgrade. Later, the sword was moved again,

Count Jelačić, mounted on horseback, watches over the lively square named after him

Fuit and vegetable stalls in the atmospheric Dolac market

pointing directly southwards to the Serbian-held capital at Knin during the war against the Republic of the Serbian Krajina in the 1990s.

These days, tourists pose for photos next to the statue and locals arrange to meet beneath the nearby clock. This is a good place to start the *korzo*, the **evening promenade** that is as much a part of Zagreb ritual as the *volta* in Athens or the *passeggiata* in Rome. Fashionably dressed teenagers, students and office workers appear magically at the same time each evening to walk, talk and flirt and above all to see and be seen. Most of the action takes place in the pedestrianised streets to the south of Trg Bana Jelačića, especially Bogovićeva and Gajeva, with their many bars and ice-cream parlours.

The Market

All around Trg Bana Jelačića are elegant examples of Vienna Secession architecture, a late 19th-century Austro-Hungarian movement broadly equivalent to Art Nouveau. A passage on the north side of the square leads to **Dolac**, the city's main market since 1930. Croatians are passionate about the quality of their fresh produce and there is nowhere better to see the range of goods available. An indoor market hall contains stalls selling bread, pasta, cheese, ham and sausages, nuts, grain and olives, while an annexe on the western side is devoted to fish. Upstairs, farmers from the surrounding countryside sell fruit, vegetables, eggs and herbs. The market is open daily from 8am, arrive early if you want to soak up the atmosphere.

 Insider Tip

TAKING A BREAK

Take your pick from the various cafés lining Trg Bana
Jelačića square. **Aida Café**, on the north side close to the
equestrian statue, is a popular choice in a prime people-
watching spot. Other good options are **Ban Café** on the
same side, **Gradska Kavana** on the northeast corner closest
to the cathedral and **Kavana Dubrovnik** on the south side
of the square. If you want something more substantial,
there are several inexpensive grill restaurants on the lower
terrace at Dolac market. Rubelj (➤ 64) has outside seating
with large parasols, a number of basic dishes to choose
from and is a popular choice for lunch.

Trg Bana Jelačića is a great place for people-watching

➕ 211 F3 🚋 Tram 1, 6, 11, 12, 13, 14, 17

Tourist Information Office
✉ Trg Bana Jelačića 11
☎ 014 814 051
🕐 Mon–Fri 8:30–8, Sat 9–6, Sun 10–4

INSIDER INFO

- The tourist information office, in the southeast corner of the square, sells the
  Zagreb Card which is well worth buying if you plan to spend a few days in the city.
  Valid for 24 or 72 hours, it gives unlimited use of all public transport in Zagreb
  (including the funicular to Gradec and the Medvednica cable car) and half-price
  entry to museums, as well as discounts at restaurants, shops, theatres and car
  rental agencies.
- **Ilica,** which runs west from Trg Bana Jelačića, is Zagreb's **principal shopping street.**
  Just off the square, the **Vincek** *slastičarnica* (pastry shop) at Ilica 18 sells some of
  the most delicious chestnut delicacies in town.

⑫ Gornji Grad

The medieval district of Gornji Grad (Upper Town), with its cobbled streets, churches and red-tiled roofs, is the most atmospheric part of the city. It was built on a hill at the end of the 11th century and is the original nucleus of Zagreb, though little remains from that period. Most of what you see today was built after 1880 when an earthquake destroyed much of the Old Town.

Gornji Grad consists of two separate settlements, divided by the dried-up riverbed of what is now Tkalčićeva. To the west is **Gradec**, the seat of government since the 17th century; to the east is **Kaptol**, the ecclesiastical capital, with its cathedral, archbishop's palace and religious institutions.

The most enjoyable way to reach the upper town is on the 🚠 **uspinjača**, a funicular tramway which takes less than a minute to make the ascent from Tomićeva. Take a seat at the lower end of the carriage to enjoy the views over Donji Grad as you climb. The blue-painted funicular has been operating since 1893 and has become a much-loved feature of Zagreb. It departs every 10 minutes between 6:30am and midnight, so you shouldn't have long to wait. Children in particular love this rattling means of transport.

Gradec
Kula Lotrščak (Burglars' Tower), opposite the upper funicular terminus, is the only surviving part of Gradec's 13th-century fortifications. It is named after the bell called *campana latrunculorum*, the 'bell of thieves' which once chimed each night before the closing of the city gates. The tower

The Lotrščak tower in Gornji Grad

was rebuilt in the mid-19th century, with a spiral staircase leading to an observation gallery; since that time it has been used as a warehouse, wine cellar, café and billiards club. Those of a nervous disposition should keep away at midday, when a cannon is fired from the tower. It was first used on New Year's Day 1877 as a signal for the city's bell-ringers and the citizens of Zagreb soon learned to set their watches by the sound of the Grič cannon.

A short distance from here, **Trg Svetog Marka** (St Mark's Square) is the focal point of Gradec. At its heart is **St Mark's Church**, the oldest parish church in Zagreb. The church is notable for its mosaic roof tiles which date from 1882 and feature the historic coats of arms of Croatia (the red and white chequerboard, still found in the national flag), Dalmatia (three lions), Slavonia (a pine marten running between the rivers Sava and Drava) and Zagreb (a castle). Inside the church you will find a number of sculptures by Ivan Meštrović, including a crucifixion scene and a Madonna with Child. On either side of the square stand the most powerful political institutions in Croatia – the **Sabor** (Croatian parliament), where independence from Yugoslavia was declared in 1991 and the **Banski Dvori** (Governor's Palace) which now houses the presidential offices.

From the east side of St Mark's Square, Ulica Kamenita leads to the **Kamenita Vrata** (Stone Gate) which dates from the 13th century and is the only survivor of the four original entrances to Gradec. When a fire in 1731 destroyed most of the nearby buildings, an image of the Virgin Mary was found in the ashes and a chapel was built to house it inside the restored gate. More recently, this has become an important place of pilgrimage. Nuns sell votive candles from a small shop next to the shrine and the air is heavy with the smell of incense and dripping wax.

The colourful roof is certainly the most eye-catching element of St. Mark's seen from outside

Kaptol

From here it is a short walk to Kaptol, dominated by the neo-Gothic twin spires of its **cathedral.** The first church dated from around 1102, but was later destroyed and rebuilt in the Gothic style. Following the 1880 earthquake, the cathedral was rebuilt yet again, this time by the German architect Hermann Bollé.

The biggest draw is the **sarcophagus of Cardinal Alojzije Stepinac** (1898–1960), a former archbishop of Zagreb who was accused of collaborating with the fascist Ustaše regime and was subsequently jailed and placed under house arrest by Tito. Since independence in 1991, he has become a Croatian national hero and was beatified by the Pope on a visit to Croatia in 1998. His tomb is usually surrounded by visitors paying their respects. Note also the relief by Ivan Meštrović in the north wall, showing Stepinac kneeling before Christ. Behind this, in the sacristy, there are several 13th-century frescoes.

The column outside the cathedral is topped by a gilded statue of the Virgin surrounded by angels, the work of the Viennese sculptor Anton Fernkorn (1813–78) who also designed the statue of Governor Jelačić in Trg Bana Jelačića.

TAKING A BREAK

The cafés on Katarinin Trg, near Lotrščak Tower, are a good place to enjoy a relaxing drink outside. For lunch, eat *al fresco* in the garden or on the terrace of **Pod Gričkim Topom** (➤ 64), or sample the excellent fish dishes served in the Gault-Millau award-winning restaurant **Ribarski brevijar** (Kaptol 27, tel: 014 829 999, Mon–Sat 1–1, ££).

Kula Lotrščak
🕂 211 E4 ✉ Strossmayerovo Šetalište 9
☎ 014 851 768
🕐 Mon–Fri 9am–5pm, Sat/Sun 10am–3pm 🖐 20kn

Katedrala (cathedral)
🕂 211 F4 ✉ Kaptol 31
☎ 014 814 727
🕐 Daily 10–6 🖐 Free

INSIDER INFO

- Take a stroll along **Strossmayerovo Šetalište**, a promenade next to the upper station of the *uspinjača* that follows the line of the old city walls, with benches, shady walkways and views across the rooftops of Donji Grad to the tower blocks of Novi Zagreb, beyond the River Sava in the distance.
- Children will enjoy the 🔢 **Prirodoslovni Muzej**, a natural history museum housed in an old theatre at Ulica Demetrova 1 (open Tue, Fri 10–5, Sat, Sun 10–1, 20kn), with an impressive collection of stuffed animals displayed in old-fashioned cabinets.

Insider Tip

⑬ Atelijer Ivan Meštrović

This magical little museum provides an excellent introduction to the work of Ivan Meštrović (1883–1962), one of the most accomplished sculptors of the 20th century and one of the few Croatians to have become famous beyond his country's borders. Spend any amount of time in Croatia and you will soon become familiar with his work which can be seen in churches and monuments, on squares and in parks from Zagreb to Split.

Meštrović was born in Slavonia to a family of itinerant agricultural workers. Despite a lack of formal education – he had to teach himself to read and write – his artistic ability was soon spotted and, at the age of fifteen, he was apprenticed to a stonemason in Split. Later he studied in Vienna and worked in Paris and Rome where he came into contact with the French sculptor Auguste Rodin (1840–1917). By 1905 he had produced *Well of Life*, a group of bronze figures around a fountain which is now on display outside the Croatian National Theatre.

After two decades abroad, Meštrović returned to Croatia and settled in this 17th-century building in Zagreb that now accommodates the museum. This is where he lived and worked from 1924 to 1942. As an active campaigner for Croat-Serb unity, he was imprisoned by the fascist Ustaše government. He spent his later life in exile in the United States where he took up a professorship for sculpture at the University of Notre Dame in the state of Indiana. He died there in 1962.

With much of the artist's furniture on display, the house retains the atmosphere of a family home. The main attraction, however, is the collection of over 100 of his sculptures in wood, bronze and stone, representing some forty years of his

HIGHLIGHTS

- *Woman in Agony* (1928): this contorted nude figure, sculpted in bronze, stands in the middle of the atrium, a small courtyard entered from the street before going into the museum.
- *History of the Croats* (1932): this bronze sculpture in the musum garden is full of political symbolism, featuring a mother as the emblem of the nation holding a stone tablet inscribed in Glagolitic script (➤ 179) on her lap.
- *Mother and Child* (1942): on display in the artist's studio, this beautiful, unfinished carving in walnut shows the tender features of a mother embracing her child.
- *Olga Meštrović feeding Tvrtko* (1925): an intimate portrait of Meštrović's second wife breast-feeding their young child, it has a Madonna-like quality.

above: Bronze sculpture *Woman in Agony* in the Fondacija Ivan Meštrović

left: Bust of Ivan Meštrović (1883–1962)

work and providing a good overview of his style which combined elements of classical sculpture and folk art. The most common themes are religious imagery and female nudes, though there are also some touching portraits of his family.

TAKING A BREAK

Konoba Didov San (Ulica Mletačka 11, tel: 014 851 154), across the street, serves inexpensive Croatian meals.

➕ 211 E4 ✉ Ulica Mletačka 8 ☎ 014 851 123
🕐 Tue–Fri 10–6, Sat–Sun 10–2 💰 20kn

INSIDER INFO

Although the major works are exhibited in the ground-floor studio and garden, take time to explore the **first-floor galleries.** Among the items on display are some plaster reliefs of the artist's parents, children and first wife, designed for the family mausoleum in Otavice, near Split. The original bronze doors of the mausoleum were looted by Serbian troops during their occupation of Croatia in the 1990s, making these surviving copies all the more significant.

Insider Tip

At Your Leisure

Muzej Grada in Zagreb is filled with interesting exhibits

🔟 Muzej Grada Zagreba

You could easily spend a couple of hours in the absorbing **Museum of the City of Zagreb,** full of maps, photographs, scale models and artefacts to explain the history of Zagreb from its foundation in 1094 to the present day. It is housed in the **17th-century Convent** of the Poor Clares, along with the medieval Popov Turen (Priests' Tower) and an adjacent granary and school.

From the street with its *trompe-l'oeil* painted windows which only serve to emphasise the seclusion of the enclosed order of nuns that once lived here, you enter through the courtyard, most notable for the fine sundial on its façade.

A recent renovation has uncovered various archaeological remains in the basement and a tour of the museum begins with a walk through a reconstruction of a metal workshop from the 1st century BC. From here, you leap forward 1,000 years for an enjoyable tour of Zagreb's history, arranged chronologically, but with some galleries devoted to themes such as shopping, theatres and parks.

Among the objects to look out for are the oldest known coat of arms of Zagreb, carved in stone in 1499, the original 17th-century stone figures of Jesus, Mary, the apostles and the archangel Gabriel from the cathedral portal, a set of brightly painted 'targets' awarded as prizes in competitions organised by the Zagreb shooting club, the city's first civic society, established in 1796 and some charming reconstructed shopfronts from 19th-century Ilica.

There is a large collection of political and tourist posters from the 20th century and the final exhibit features video footage of the Serbian attack on the presidential palace in 1991, together with broken crockery and furniture.

Stara Vura (Old Clock), the restaurant in the museum's vaulted stone basement is unfortunately closed indefinitely.

➕ 211 E5 ✉ Ulica Opatička 20 ☎ 014 851 364 🕐 Tue, Fri 10–6, Sat 11–7, Sun 10–2 💷 30kn

🔟 Hrvatski Muzej Naivne Umjetnosti

This small museum gives a good introduction to the **Croatian Naïve Art movement.** Originating in the 1930s when a group of villagers in Hlebine (➤ 85) began painting vivid scenes of rural life on glass, the two key figures in the movement were Ivan Generalić (1914–92) and Franjo Mraz (1910–81). Before long there was a whole group of artists known as the Hlebine School. These were self-taught, peasant artists who drew what they saw and their early work reflected scenes of everyday rural life. In time, the movement developed and became known internationally; the later generation of naïve artists, while similar in style, used greater technical complexity and their work became influenced by Surrealism and Magical Realism.

The museum features an overview of naïve art from the 1930s onwards, with an emphasis on the Hlebine School, but also including artists from Dalmatia and abroad. The first room is devoted to Generalić; it is interesting to compare his *Self-Portrait* (1975) with the contemporary portrait of *Father Fishing* (1974) by his son Josip (1936–2004). The first works of Croatian naïve sculpture, including wooden figures of Adam and Eve and *Mother and Child* by Petar Smajić (1910–85) are also displayed here.

➕ 211 E4 ✉ Ulica Svetog Ćirila i Metoda 3 ☎ 014 851 911 🕐 Tue–Fri 10–6, Sat–Sun 10–1 💷 20kn

🔟 Muzej Za Umjetnost i Obrt

The wide-ranging **Arts and Crafts Museum** is housed in a late 19th-century building designed by Hermann Bollé (1845–1916), the architect of the cathedral and

Mirogoj cemetery (➤ 60). It was founded immediately following the earthquake of 1880 to preserve traditional works of art and craft in the face of the new threat of mass production.

The museum's collections of painting, sculpture, clocks, musical instruments, furniture, silverware and graphic design offers a broad sweep through the arts and it is easy to get overwhelmed, but it is manageable if you concentrate on a few key themes.

The highlight of the first floor is the sacred art collection, with altarpieces from northern Croatian churches (note the 17th-century Madonna from the village of Remetinec) and a number of statues from Zagreb cathedral.

The second-floor galleries feature Art Nouveau, art deco and 20th-century art and design, showing how Croatian art has developed alongside mainstream European trends.

➕ 211 D2 ✉ Trg Maršala Tita 10 ☎ 014 882 111 🕐 Tue, Sat 10–7, Sun 10–2 💷 30kn

🔟 Muzej Mimara

Zagreb's biggest museum is based entirely on the **personal collection** of the Croatian businessman Ante

This impressive statue outside Muzej Za Umjetnost i Obrt depicts the story of George and the Dragon

Zagreb

The Bather by Renoir in the Muzej Mimara

Topić Mimara (1898–1987) who made his fortune abroad and spent it amassing art works which he donated to the nation shortly before his death.

Room 1 contains some of the oldest objects, including a Christian chalice from Alexandria dating from the 3rd century AD, acquired by Mimara at the age of nineteen and said to have been the catalyst for his life-long love affair with collecting. Among other highlights are a 14th-century carved ivory English hunting horn (Room 17), an ivory sceptre used by Polish kings (Room 26), *Virgin with the Innocents* by Rubens and *Portrait of a Lady* by Rembrandt (Room 35) and a sensual portrait: *The Bather* by Renoir (Room 40). If you need a break to recharge your batteries, there is a café on the ground floor.

➕ 211 D2 ✉ Rooseveltov Trg 4
☎ 014 828 100 ⏰ Tue–Wed, Fri–Sat 10–5, Thu 10–7, Sun 10–2 💰 40kn

18 Etnografski Muzej

The last in the trio of museums on the western side of the 'Green Horseshoe' (➤ panel below) is devoted to folk culture, both in Croatia and elsewhere. The ground-floor gallery of the Ethnographic Museum features objects brought back from abroad by Croatian explorers, notably the brothers **Mirko and Stjepan Seljan.** Of greater interest are the first-floor displays of folk costume and jewellery from the various regions of Croatia, along with a number of traditional musical instruments. The museum is housed in a magnificent congress hall, dating from 1904, with beautiful stained glass, sculptures on the façade and frescoes in the central dome.

➕ 211 D2 ✉ Trg Mažuranića 14
☎ 014 826 220 ⏰ Tue–Thu 10–6, Fri–Sun 10–1 💰 15kn

THE GREEN HORSESHOE

Glance at a map of *Donji Grad* (Lower Town) and you will easily make out the Green Horseshoe, a U-shaped promenade of interconnected parks and squares designed by Milan Lenuci (1849–1924). The aim was to provide a green lung for the expanding city, with parks for relaxation, along with handsome buildings housing the museums, art galleries and theatres where citizens could spend their leisure time. Although the horseshoe was never completed, two major sections still exist today. The first begins on Trg Nikole Šubića Zrinskog and continues south to the equestrian statue of King Tomislav on Trg Kralja Tomislava, passing through Strossmayerova Trg, where you can find the Strossmayerova Galerija Starih Majstora (Strossmayer Gallery of Old Masters). A parallel section begins by the Hrvatsko Narodno Kazalište (Croatian National Theatre) on Trg Maršala Tita and leads south past the Ethnographic Museum towards the Botanički Vrt (Botanical Garden), an English-style landscape garden laid out in 1889.

🔢 Arheološki Muzej

Spread out over three floors of a 19th-century Habsburg palace, this archaeological museum has a comprehensive collection of finds from prehistoric to Roman times, but the biggest attraction is the **Vučedol Dove**, a three-legged pouring vessel in the shape of a bird dating from the third millennium BC. The vessel probably served some religious or ceremonial function, such as anointing with oil. It is the finest surviving example of grooved pottery, decorated with geometric patterns, that was a hallmark of the Vučedol culture around Vukovar in eastern Croatia more than 4000 years ago. Since the siege of Vukovar in 1991, the Vučedol Dove has become a powerful symbol of peace, reproduced on the 20-kuna banknote. Also on display is the **Zagreb Mummy**, brought back from Egypt in 1848. It was wrapped in a linen shroud from the 4th-century BC containing the world's longest example of the Etruscan language – an ancient text still to be deciphered. Don't miss the lapidarium in the museum courtyard, with Roman stone monuments and a café.

🔶 211 F3 ✉ Trg Nikole Šubića Zrinskog 19 ☎ 014 873 101 🕐 Tue, Wed, Fri 10–5, Sat 10–6 💷 20kn

A capuchin monkey enjoys a tasty piece of fruit in the zoo in Maksimir Park (➤ 60)

Zagreb

20 🍴 Maksimirski Perivoj

The residents of Zagreb flock to Maksimir Park, one of the oldest public parks in Europe, on weekend afternoons to stroll, ride bicycles, feed the swans, take the kids to play on the swings or relax on the grass. Footpaths, lakes, bridges, follies and a belvedere café all help to create an enjoyable retreat, a short tram ride from the city. A 🍴 zoo houses native species such as brown bears and wolves, as well as elephants, lions, tigers, chimpanzees, crocodiles, an aquarium and a reptile house.
➕ 211 off F3 🚋 Tram 11, 12

ZOO
☎ 012 302 199 ⏰ Daily 9–8, in summer, 9–5, in winter 💷 30kn

21 🍴 Medvednica

Insider Tip
The wooded slopes of Medvednica (Bear Mountain) offer the nearest thing to a wilderness experience and make an excellent day-trip from Zagreb. Take tram no. 8 or 14 to the Mihaljevac terminus, from where you can take buses to the summit. A cable car that first started operating in 1963 was closed in 2007, a new one is however being planned. Buses go as far as the Tomislavov Dom hotel, from where the peak of **Sljeme** (1035m/3395ft) can be reached in just a few minutes. At the top there is a television tower and a viewing platform with wonderful panoramic views over Zagreb to the south and Zagorje (➤ 75) to the north. Ski lifts operate in winter. Sljeme is not Croatia's only ski resort but its best known and especially child-friendly one. It was here that the Croatian brother-and-sister alpine skiers Ivica and Janica Kostelić first learnt to ski.

From the summit of Sljeme there are numerous waymarked walks through the beech woods. For a pleasant hike of several hours turn right at the upper cable-car station and follow signs to Puntijarka until you reach a large steep meadow.

Shortly afterwards you will come to the Church of Our Lady of Sljeme, built in 1932 at an altitude of 1000m (3280ft) to celebrate 1000 years of Christianity in Croatia. Stay on this path as far as the Puntijarka mountain shelter (➤ 64), then follow trail no. 18 back down to Dolje through the woods.
➕ 211 off F5 ⏰ Buses: Sat/Sun 8am–8.40pm every 1hr 30mins

22 Groblje Mirogoj

Take the bus to Mirogoj from in front of the cathedral and you will probably be joined by widows carrying flowers and candles to put on their husbands' graves – a reminder that this is a real cemetery, not just a museum piece.

Designed by the ubiquitous Hermann Bollé in 1876, it lies behind a long, ivy-covered wall topped with green domes. Most impressive are the neo-Renaissance arcades to either side of the main entrance with mosaic-tiled floors and elaborate funereal monuments marking the tombs of Croatia's aristocratic families.

Halfway along the arcade to the right, look out for the tomb of Stjepan Radić (1871–1928), the leader of the Croatian Peasants Party and advocate of independence who was shot dead in the Belgrade parliament in 1928. The first president of Croatia, Franjo Tuđman (1922–99), occupies a grandiose black granite tomb behind the main chapel. It's just as interesting to wander among the rows of ordinary graves, where Catholic, Orthodox, Jewish, Muslim and Communist citizens lie buried side by side, the symbols on their tombstones illustrating clearly that this is a cemetery for all the people of Zagreb.
➕ 211 off F5
⏰ Daily 7.30–6 🚌 106

The richly decorated neo-Renaissance arcades in Mirogoj cemetery

Where to...
Stay

Prices
Expect to pay per person per night for a double room in summer:
£ under 300kn   **££** 300kn–600kn   **£££** over 600kn

Dubrovnik ££
Built in 1929, the Dubrovnik is most notable for its rippling glass façade which looks down over the pedestrianised shopping streets to the south of Trg Bana Jelačića. Some of the 260 rooms overlook the main square, all have air-conditioning and satellite TV. Although this hotel does not have the atmosphere of others in this price category, it is centrally located, with the buzzing café life of Bogovićeva just a few feet away.
➕ 211 D3 ✉ Ulica Ljudevita Gaja 1 ☎ 014 863 555; www.hotel-dubrovnik.hr 🚋 Tram 1, 6, 11, 12, 13, 14, 17

Esplanade Zagreb £££
Those who like a bit of style stay at the Esplanade that was built in 1925 especially for guests arriving on the Orient Express. The gardens with their fountains and the Art Nouveau entrance hall are a reminder of times long past. After extensive renovation, the hotel now has modern offices, WiFi Internet, a fitness club and casino. Marble bathrooms, for example, make a stay in one of the 208 rooms absolutely luxurious. The botanical garden is just a few minutes walk away.
➕ 211 F1 ✉ Ulica Mihanovićeva 1 ☎ 014 566 666; www.esplanade.hr 🚋 tram lines 2, 4, 6, 9, 13

Ilica ££
This small, friendly hotel is set just back from a busy shopping street, a 15-minute walk from Trg Bana Jelačića. There are 20 cosy rooms with private bathrooms and the corridors are decorated with impressions of Zagreb by local artists. Ilica is the best mid-range option in central Zagreb and it tends to get booked up, so book well in advance. Contrary to information circulated in other travel forums, the hotel does accept credit cards.

Insider Tip

➕ 211 off D3 ✉ Ilica 102 ☎ 013 777 522; www.hotel-ilica.hr 🚋 Tram 1, 6, 11

Palace £££
The *grande dame* among Zagreb's hotels was built as the Schlessinger Palace in 1891 and converted to a hotel in 1907 – the city's first hotel. Despite renovation work, it has retained its old-world atmosphere and antique style and oozes Art Nouveau charm. Many of the rooms look over Strossmayerova Trg, a leafy square at the heart of the green corridor connecting the railway station with Trg Bana Jelačića.
➕ 211 F2 ✉ Strossmayerov Trg 10 ☎ 014 899 600; www.palace.hr 🚋 Trams 6, 13

Sliško ££
This small, modern, family-run hotel makes a convenient choice for anyone arriving by bus as it is just 200m (220 yards) from the bus station and the airport bus terminus. There are 18 simply furnished rooms with private bathrooms and satellite TV. It stands on a quiet road, a 15-minute tram ride from Trg Bana Jelačića. Free WiFi – Internet access that works everywhere in the building.
➕ 211 off F1 ✉ Bunićeva 7 ☎ 016 184 777; www.slisko.hr 🚋 Trams 2, 5, 6, 7, 8

Where to...
Eat and Drink

Prices
Expect to pay for a starter, main course, salad and house wine or water for one:
£ under 100kn   **££** 100kn–200kn   **£££** over 200kn

Baltazar ££

This long-established restaurant just north of the cathedral serves a classic menu of grilled meat dishes such as steaks, chops and burgers with a choice of chips, roasted peppers or potato balls with gorgonzola. It can get busy, so reserve in advance, especially if you want a table in the courtyard. If you have a Zagreb Card, remember to claim your 10 percent discount. On the same site are Gašpar, a fish restaurant and Melkior, a wine bar.

➕ 211 F5 **✉** Nova Ves 4 **☎** 014 666 999
🕐 Mon–Sat noon–midnight **🚌** Bus 106

Boban ££

The footballer Zvonimir Boban, the captain of Croatia's 1998 World Cup squad, opened this Italian restaurant in a brick-vaulted cellar just off the main square. Fresh pasta is a speciality here, with spaghetti, tortellini, ravioli and gnocchi prepared in a variety of ways, along with *carpaccio* of beef or tuna and Italian-inspired salads and risottos. The restaurant and the bar attract a young, trendy crowd.

➕ 211 F3 **✉** Ulica Ljudevita Gajeva 9
☎ 014 811 549
🕐 Mon–Thu 11–11, Fri, Sat 11am–midnight, Sun noon–11 **🚋** Tram 1, 6, 11, 12, 13, 14, 17

Ivica i Marica ££

Ivica and Marica are Croatia's Hansel and Gretel and this enjoyable restaurant on Zagreb's main bar-hopping strip combines a fairy-tale cottage atmosphere with light, healthy organic and vegetarian cuisine. There are a few meat and fish dishes, including trout from rivers in the Žumberak region, but most people stick to vegetarian choices such as wholemeal pasta and *štrukli* (baked pastry parcels with cheese and spinach). However, if you just want a snack, choose from the delectable selection of home-made cakes in the bakery next door.

➕ 211 F4 **✉** Tkalčićeva 70 **☎** 014 817 321
🕐 Daily noon–11

Kerempuh ££

This busy restaurant on the upper level of Dolac market attracts a mixed crowd of market workers, shoppers, business people and tourists, so try to arrive early for a lunchtime seat on the terrace. The menu changes daily according to what is available in the market, so the food is ultra-fresh and you have a prime view of the activity going on beneath you. The main emphasis is on meat dishes such as *pašticada*, a casserole of veal stewed in wine and served with mashed potatoes. Stuffed cabbage is another speciality at Kerempuh.

➕ 211 F4 **✉** Kaptol 3 **☎** 014 819 000
🕐 Mon–Sat 9–3, 7–11, Sun 9–4
🚋 Trams 1, 6, 11, 12, 13, 14, 17

Korčula ££

Only one block south of the heart of Zagreb's café society, this is a well-regarded traditional restaurant that's smart enough to feel like dining out without any of the formalities. Foodwise, Korčula has a high-quality Dalmatian menu that is strong on seafood – fresh Adriatic

Insider Tip

fish served with *blitva*, octopus prepared in a *peka* – but also has room for rich beef stew *pasčticada*.

➕ 211 F3 ✉ Nikole Tesle 17 ☎ 014 872 159
🕐 Mon–Sat 11–11

Pod Gričkim Topom ££

Pod Gričkim Topom, which means 'under the Grič cannon', makes the perfect setting for a romantic meal. The attentive staff at this flower-decked terrace overlooking Zagreb, a few steps from Lotršćak Tower, are fluent in several languages and will bring you a small starter on the house. Afterwards, you could try Zagorje soup, a hearty broth of ham, cheese, bacon, mushrooms and potatoes. The main menu is heavy on grilled fish and expertly cooked steaks, such as *zagrebački odrezak*, a veal schnitzel stuffed with ham and cheese. If you use the WC, the key symbol is for men and the keyhole is for women.

Insider Tip

➕ 211 E4 ✉ Zakmardijeve Stube 5 (near the upper funicular station) ☎ 014 833 607
🕐 Mon–Sat 11am–midnight
🚡 Funicular to Gradec

Puntijarka £

An easy 45-minute walk from the bus stop at the upper cable-car station leads to this mountain hut on the slopes of Medvednica (Bear Mountain). There are no frills here, just good, hearty fare such as *grah* (bean stew), roast pork and *purica z mlincima* (turkey with pasta), served at outdoor tables in summer or in the snug alpine lodge in winter. A path next to the restaurant leads down towards the tram terminus at Dolje. Come up to Puntijarka by bus for lunch and then walk back down in a couple of hours.

➕ 211 off F5 ✉ Sljemenska Cesta 4
☎ 014 580 384 🕐 Daily 9–9

Rubelj £

Rubelj is the busiest of several grill restaurants on a terrace beneath Dolac market, with enticing outdoor tables and giant parasols. The menu features kebabs, hamburgers, sausages and mixed grills, served with a selection of crusty bread, raw onions and *ajvar* (aubergine and pepper relish). Steaks, pizzas, grilled squid, salad and chips are all available, but most people go for the *čevapčići*. This restaurant is a great place for a light, snack lunch, right in the heart of town.

➕ 201 D3 ✉ Dolac 2 ☎ 014 818 777
🕐 Daily 8am–11pm 🚋 Trams 1, 6, 11–14, 17

Tač £££

A popular destination on Vrhovec, 5km (3.1mi) from the centre, the restaurant's much praised cuisine upholds the traditions of Istria and Slavonia. In spring, you will find wild asparagus on the menu, in autumn truffles and even Istrian Boškarin beef that can only be served in specially licenced restaurants, or Slavonian *kulen* sausage and *štrukli* from the Zagorje region. The Tač family buy directly from regional producers and everything is freshly prepared. Cosy, rustic restaurant and tables outside make a visit here a pleasure at any time of year. The restaurant can be reached by car or on foot.

Insider Tip

➕ 211 off D5 ✉ Vrhovec 140 ☎ 013 776 757
🕐 Tue–Sun noon–midnight

Vallis Aurea £

A little piece of Slavonia in the heart of Zagreb, Vallis Aurea lies at the foot of the funicular that leads to Gradec. The wooden tables and embroidered tablecloths give the restaurant a cosy, intimate atmosphere. The food is spicy, with starters such as ham and horse-radish, smoked ox tongue or *kulen* (Slavonian salami) and there are always three good-value daily specials ranging from boiled beef to fish stew – or simply enjoy a glass of chilled Slavonian wine outside on the summer terrace.

➕ 211 E4 ✉ Ulica Tomića 4
☎ 014 831 305 🕐 Mon–Sat 9am–11pm
🚋 Trams 1, 6, 11, 12, 13, 14, 17

Where to...
Shop

Shopping in Zagreb has come a long way since the days of Communist Yugoslavia and the city now has a variety of department stores, fashion boutiques and shopping malls.

SHOPPING DISTRICTS

The main shopping areas are all close to Trg Bana Jelačića. **Ilica,** which runs west of Trg Bana Jelačića for some 7km (4mi), has been the city's main commercial street since the 19th century and now boasts shops selling antiques, clothing and shoes. **Vlaška,** which begins near the cathedral and continues east, offers a similar mixture.

For more alternative shopping, **Radićeva** and **Tkalčićeva,** running uphill from the northwest corner of Trg Bana Jelačića, have funky, off-beat, designer boutiques and quirky art galleries and craft shops. **Gallery Gea** (Radićeva 35) specialises in carnival masks, while **Art Club Suveniri** (Radićeva 31) has a wide range from T-shirts to carvings.

SHOPPING CENTRES

Many of Zagreb's smarter shops are in shopping centres rather than on the main streets. Among the biggest are the historic department store **Nama** (Ilica 4), **Centar Kaptol** (Nova Ves 17), **Importanne** (Starčevićev Trg, outside the railway station) and **Importanne Galleria** (Iblerov Trg, near Vlaška).

The more modern centres, such as **Centar Kaptol** and **Importanne Galleria** (open Mon–Sat 9–9, some open Sundays), resemble American-style shopping malls, with eateries, multiplex cinemas and shops.

FOOD AND DRINK

For fresh produce, you can't beat the **farmers' market** which takes place every morning at Dolac, just off Trg Bana Jelačića.

Since 1902, **Blato** has been a synonym for fresh ham (*pršut*), olive oil, wine and other regional delicacies, including the famous sheep's cheese from Pag (*paški sir*). Shops can also be found in the market hall at **Dolac** (Selska cesta 56).

A short walk east of the cathedral, **Franja** (Vlaška 62) sells fresh coffee and tea, plus a wide selection of wines and liqueurs. There is another branch of **Franja** on Heinzelova 6b. **Vinoteka Bornstein** (Kaptol 19) is the place to go for Croatian wine and it has a second outlet at Pantovčak 9. **Natura Croatica** (Preradovićeva 8) sell tempting honeys, jams and liqueurs, among other things.

FASHIONS

Heruc Galerija (Ilica 26) and **Image Haddad** (Ilica 6) are high-street chains offering affordable, stylish women's clothes. For something more glamorous, head for **Gharani Štrok** (Dezmanova 5), owned by a London-based Croatian fashion designer. **Croata** (Ilica 5 and Kaptol 13) is the place to pick up a Croatian silk tie for the man in your life.

OTHER SHOPS

Algoritam (Ulica Ljudevita Gaja 1), beneath Hotel Dubrovnik, is the top bookshop in town, with foreign-language books and magazines.

Aromatéka (Heinzelova 2) is the place to go for cosmetics and soaps made naturally from Adriatic herbs.

Zagreb

Where to...
Go Out

Zagreb has a thriving arts scene and with numerous theatres, cinemas, concert halls and orchestras, there is something going on throughout the year.

To find out what's on, pick up a copy of the monthly *Events and Performances* leaflet from the tourist office on Trg Bana Jelačića, or look at their website (www.zagreb-touristinfo.hr). Another good source of information is the magazine *Zagreb in your Pocket*, available free from tourist offices, cafés and hotels (www.inyourpocket.com).

In summer, a variety of different events are held outside, e.g. **folk-dancing** on Trg Bana Jelačića during the **International Folklore Festival** in July and concerts in the music pavilion on Trg Nikole Šubića Zrinskog. The annual **Zagreb Summer Evenings** festival includes chamber music concerts in the cathedral as well as other events.

THEATRE AND MUSIC

The most prestigious venue for plays, ballets and operas is the **Hrvatsko Narodno Kazalište** (Croatian National Theatre, tel: 014 888 415; www.hnk.hr) – an ostentatious, Habsburg-era opera house on Trg Maršala Tita opened by Emperor Franz Josef I in 1895. The theatre is home to the National Ballet and National Opera, but also plays host to visiting companies throughout the year. The box office is open Monday to Friday 10–7:30, Saturday 10–1, as well as 90 minutes before performances.

The other major venue is the **Vatroslav Lisinski Concert Hall** at Trg Stjepan Radića 4 (tel: 016 121 166; www.lisinski.hr). Home to the Zagreb Philharmonic Orchestra, it also features jazz and other musical events.

Children might enjoy the shows performed at the **Zagrebačko Kazalište Lutaka** (Zagreb Puppet Theatre) on Trg Kralja Tomislava.

CINEMA

Most major international films are shown shortly after their release, usually with subtitles. Two good central cinemas are **Cineplexx** in the Centar Kaptol shopping centre and the **cinematic art club** at Trg žrtava fašizma 14. Listings of what is on can be found in the daily newspapers.

NIGHTLIFE

For most locals, a night out, especially in summer, means finding a café and sitting out on the street. The most popular streets are Radićeva and Tkalčićeva north of Trg Bana Jelačića and Gajeva and Bogovićeva to the south. The established place for serious clubbers is **Aquarius** (www.apuarius.hr), on the shores of Lake Jarun, 4km (2.5mi) south of the city. For live music, head for **Sax** at Palmotićeva 22 (tel: 014 872 836; www.sax-zg.hr).

FOOTBALL

Croatia's top football team, Dinamo Zagreb (http://gnkdinamo.hr), plays in **Maksimir Stadium** opposite Maksimir Park which is also the venue for home games for the Croatian national team. Matches generally take place between August and May. Check for tickets in advance (tel: 012 386 125).

Inland Croatia

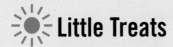 **Little Treats**

A relaxed summer's day

Just do as the residents of **Varaždin** (➤ 78) do and spend a lazy few hours on the banks of the Drau.

Mixing with the Croats

Once reason for a Sunday excursion into the Zagorje region is to have lunch in **Grešna Gorica** (➤ 89) together with the locals and their extended families.

The atrocities of war

A visit to the memorial and cemetery in **Vukovar** (➤ 85) is a saddening experience but makes one pause for thought.

Getting Your Bearings

Although most visitors to Croatia tend to stay in Zagreb and
around the coast, to do so is to ignore about half of the country.
The regions to the north, south and east of Zagreb offer a beguiling
mixture of scenery, historic towns and authentic rural life.
Travelling around inland Croatia is not always easy – there are
no fast roads, facilities are basic and the effects of the war years
between 1991 and 1995 can be emotionally wearing.

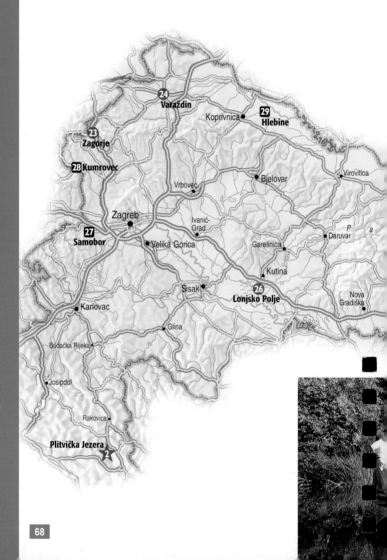

Getting Your Bearings

The rivers Sava, Drava and Danube form natural borders with Bosnia, Hungary and Serbia, separating Croatia from its neighbours. During the 16th century, the Habsburg emperors established a military frontier ('Vojna Krajina') along the Bosnian border in order to defend Croatia from the Ottoman Empire. Since 1699, this has taken in large parts of Croatia along the borders to territories in Bosnia and Serbia ruled by the Ottoman Empire. In the 1990s, this same border became a battleground and the scars of the recent war are still evident in towns such as Osijek, Slavonski Brod and Vukovar in particular. Slavonia, in the north east of Croatia, is virtually untouched by tourism. Vineyards, wheat fields and rural villages dominate the countryside. This region is famous for its rustic fare too which includes spicy salami, goulash and fish stew.

Donji Miholjac

Kopački Rit **25**

30 Osijek

Našice

Vinkovci

31 Vukovar

32 Đakovo

Požega

Slavonski Brod

Županja

0   50 km
0   30 mi

Visitors to Plitvice National Park on a boat tour on one of the lakes

Inland Croatia

Four Perfect Days

If you're not quite sure where to begin, this itinerary recommends an enjoyable four-day tour of inland Croatia, taking in some of the best places to see. For more information see the main entries (➤ 72).

Day 1

Morning

Make an early start to explore ⭐**Plitvička Jezera** (left, ➤ 72). You could easily spend all day here, but you'll need a few hours if you want to walk to Veliki Slap waterfall and take a boat trip across Lake Kozjak.

Afternoon and evening

Head north along the old main road from Split to Zagreb where several rustic roadside restaurants offer spit-roast lamb and pork. Arriving at Karlovac, take the minor road to Jastrebarsko and drive over the hills to spend the night in **27 Samobor** (➤ 84). If you still have some room, the cafés around the main square serve *kremšnita* (vanilla and custard cream cake).

Day 2

Morning

Take the motorway towards Zagreb, then north to Zabok to begin a circuit of the Zagorje region with the small museum village of **28 Kumrovec** (➤ 84).

Afternoon and evening

After lunch at Grešna Gorica (➤ 89) you should just have time to visit the **23 Zagorje** castles of Veliki Tabor and Trakošćan (right, ➤ 75) before continuing to the Baroque town of **24 Varaždin** (➤ 78). Take an evening stroll around the Old Town and have a drink in the main square before a slap-up dinner at **Verglec** (➤ 89).

Day 3

Morning
It takes about three hours to drive across the Pannonian plain from Varaždin, though you could break the journey with a visit to the galleries of Naïve Art in **29 Hlebine** (►84).

Afternoon and evening
Arriving in **30 Osijek** (►85) head straight for **25 Kopački Rit** Nature Park (►80) and book a boat trip to see herons and cormorants on the Danube flood plains. Spend the night in the nearby village of Bilje (Mala Kuća, ►87) and treat yourself to some spicy Slavonian stew at Kod Varge (►89).

Day 4

Morning
Spend an hour wandering around Tvrđa, the 18th-century fortress on the outskirts of Osijek, then head south to **32 Đakovo** (►86) to see the magnificent cathedral.

Afternoon and evening
Join the main Zagreb-Belgrade motorway for the fast journey to Novska, drive south to Jasenovac, the entry point to **26 Lonjsko Polje** Nature Park (right, ►82). Spend the the day exploring the villages inside the park, then stay in a wooden hut in Mužilovčica (►87) for the night.

Inland Croatia

★2 Plitvička Jezera

The Plitvice Lakes are undoubtedly inland Croatia's top tourist attraction, seen by more than 600,000 visitors a year. In 1949 the entire area was declared Croatia's first national park and, in 1979, it was given UNESCO World Heritage status. In summer, it is crowded with coach parties from the coastal resorts, but come out of season or early in the morning and you can have the place to yourself.

There can be no more dramatic sight in Croatia than the rushing waters of **Veliki Slap**, cascading 70m (230ft) over a limestone cliff into the **River Korana.** This is merely the culmination of a series of 16 emerald-green lakes, linked by waterfalls and subterranean water courses that drop more than 150m (490ft) over a distance of 8km (5mi). Waymarked paths and wooden bridges take you through the park.

The lakes, formed from travertine – a muddy, calcareous deposit left behind from a mixture of moss and eroded limestone – form natural barriers that cause the water level in the lakes to rise gradually. This is a rare, lush landscape in a region where rugged limestone karst is the dominant feature. Brown bears and wolves inhabit the beech, fir and spruce forests and lynx have returned.

Numerous species of butterflies, birds and wild flowers thrive here. The peaceful natural scenery is tragically at odds with the recent history of the park – it was occupied by Serb forces from 1991 to 1995 and the first people to die in the war were killed here.

👥 Seeing the lakes

It is possible to spend several days exploring the national park, staying at one of the **three on-site hotels,** but most people come just for a day trip. Even if you only have a few hours, the park is so well geared up for visitors that you can easily make the most of your time. The lakes are connected by a network of **wooden footpaths** and **bridges,** some of which pass right under and across the waterfalls, close enough to feel the spray.

With constantly changing colours and light, the Plitvice Lakes take on a different character in each season of the year. In summer, when most visitors come, they are refreshingly cool but crowded. The best times to visit are spring, when melting snows increase the flow of water and autumn, when the forests take on a gorgeous hue. In winter, when the park is almost deserted, the lakes have a special atmosphere, but they are often covered in snow and ice.

Getting around the park

The entrance ticket (valid for one day, but extendable) also includes **boat trips** and **shuttle bus services.** The maps sold

right: The lakes at Plitvička Jezera are connected by wooden footpaths and bridges

Inland Croatia

at entry points and hotels suggest a variety of itineraries from two to six hours, combining walks with free transport. In four hours, starting from Entrance 1, you could follow the blue trail to **Veliki Slap** and take a boat across the largest lake, **Jezero Kozjak**, before returning on the bus. If you have a full day, start at Entrance 2 and take a bus to **Labudovac Falls** at the head of the highest lake, Prošćansko. From here you can follow the red trail along the shores to **Jezero Kozjak** and take the boat trip downstream, saving Veliki Slap till last. With the map and the well-signed paths, it is easy to work out your own route and itinerary.

TAKING A BREAK

There are cafés by the park entrances and also near the main jetties and bus stops in the summer.

For a full meal, the rustic **Poljana** (daily 8–3) serves traditional local dishes. In winter, the only options for a place to eat are the hotels (▶89).

Breathtakingly beautiful waterfalls link the lakes

➕ 200 C4
✉ 75km (47mi) south of Karlovac
☎ 053 751 015; www.np-plitvicka-jezera.hr
🕐 summer daily 8–8 (or dusk), winter 8–3
💰 summer 110–180kn, winter 55kn

right: View of the Gothic Veliki Tabor Castle

INSIDER INFO

- If you only have a few hours, **it is worth spending the previous night in one of the on-site hotels** and making an early start before the coach parties arrive.
- The **entry fee is lower in winter,** but the boats and shuttle buses stop operating in November and the paths may be closed due to snow. However, you might catch a glimpse of Veliki Slap from the observation point near Ulaz 1.
- There are **two main entrances,** Ulaz 1 and Ulaz 2, both with car parks and information offices. Ulaz 1 is nearest to Veliki Slap, just 50m (55 yards) from an observation terrace overlooking the falls. Ulaz 2 is closer to the three hotels and makes a good starting point if you want to explore the upper lakes and waterfalls.

㉓ Zagorje

Vineyards, meadows and rolling green hills crowned by picture-postcard castles and churches – the Zagorje region north of Zagreb is one of the most attractive in Croatia.

Veliki Tabor

This 16th-century Gothic castle, built on a hill 333m (1092ft) high, completely dominates its surroundings. After a renovation programme lasting many years, it is now presented in beautiful condition both inside and outside. The basic structure is pentagonal, with four semicircular towers set around an arcaded courtyard where occasional displays of swordmanship and falconry are held. The **museum** contains a fairly dull collection of archaeological finds, but it is worth the entrance fee for the views over the Zagorje in all directions.

Trakošćan

The most visited sight in the Zagorje is the site of the original **13th-century castle,** built to defend the Bednja valley on the border to Slovenia. Trakošćan comes straight out of a fairy tale, with gleaming white walls and crenellated towers looking down over an artificial lake. The castle you see today is the result of a 19th-century restoration by the **Draškovič family,** descendants of a 16th-century noble who was granted the estate by the Habsburg emperor as a reward for fighting against the Turks. Cross the drawbridge and climb the path

---

THE STORY OF VERONIKA

The first castle at Veliki Tabor was built in the 12th century for the counts of Celje. A local tale is based on the legend of Veronica of Desinić who fell in love with the count's son and secretly eloped with him to Slovenia where they married. When she was captured, the count had her imprisoned and later ordered her to be drowned and her body walled up in the castle. A female skull was found here in 1982 – before renovation of the galleried courtyard, it was on display in the chapel – though nobody knows whether it is Veronica's.

up the wooded hillside to enter the castle, a fine example
of an aristocratic stately home with tapestries, paintings,
armour, hunting trophies, a music room, smoking and
games rooms and some splendid 18th-century braziers.

The study of the Croation painter **Julijana Erdödy-Drašković**
(1847–1901), the first recognised female painter in Croatia,
who lived here in the 19th century, can also be visited;
her original piano and easel have been preserved and
the room is decorated with her paintings of rural scenes.
After exploring the castle you can walk around the lake.
In summer there is a **lakeside café** where you can rent a
pedal-boat for a trip on the water.

Insider Tip

**Devotional
trinkets
on sale in the
pilgrimage
town of Marija
Bistrica**

MARIJA BISTRICA

While you are in the Zagorje region, visit Marija Bistrica, the **most important pilgrimage
site in Croatia.** The object of veneration here is a 15th-century dark wooden statue
of the Virgin, said to have been hidden by the priest in the walls of the parish church
to protect it from Turkish invaders and rediscovered in 1684 when a shining light
directed the bishop to its hiding place. The current church dates from 1883 and was
the work of Hermann Bollé (1845–1916), the architect of Zagreb cathedral, who
incorporated an earlier stone gateway and façade into its design. You enter through
Trg Pape Ivana Pavla II, named in honour of Pope John Paul II's visit in 1998, with
a half-cloister featuring a pair of domed pavilions and numerous marble *ex votos* or
prayers of thanks left by previous pilgrims. Climb the **Via Crucis** (Way of the Cross)
behind the church for the best views. On **religious feast days,** particularly on 15
August (Assumption) and 8 September (Birth of the Virgin), Marija Bistrica has a **fair-
ground atmosphere,** with stalls selling popcorn, balloons and gingerbread hearts and
thousands of pilgrims attending open-air mass in the auditorium behind the church.

TAKING A BREAK

Have lunch or a drink on the terrace of **Grešna Gorica** (►89) looking out over the castle at Veliki Tabor.

Stooks of
wheat in
the rural
landscape of
Zagorje

Veliki Tabor

✚ 206 B4 ☎ 049 343 963 ◉ Apr–Sep Tue–Fri 9–5, Sat/Sun 9–7, Mar, Oct Tue–Fri 9–4, Sat/Sun 9–5, Nov–Feb Tue–Sun 9–4 ✋ 20kn

Trakošćan

✚ 206 C4 ☎ 042 796 422 ◉ Summer daily 9–6, winter 9–4 ✋ 30kn

INSIDER INFO

Midway between Veliki Tabor and Trakošćan is the town of **Krapina,** best known for the discovery of *Homo Krapinensis,* a Neanderthal who lived here some 130,000 years ago. Around 900 human bones were discovered on the Hušnjakovo hill belonging to more than 20 men, women and children – the richest collection of prehistoric human remains found anywhere. The newly built 🏛 **Neanderthal Museum** (Jul, Aug Tue–Fri 9–6, Sat, Sun 9–7, Apr–Jun, Sep Tue–Sun 9–7, Mar, Oct Tue–Sun 9–6, Nov–Feb Tue–Fri 9–4, Sat, Sun 9–5, admission 25kn) includes a number of interactive elements and features reproductions of Neanderthal skulls and the full skeleton of a cave bear. You can also walk up the hill behind the museum to see where the remains were discovered.

㉔ Varaždin

The town of Varaždin is all pretty pastel shades and heavily restored façades in apricot, strawberry and vanilla, adorned with Baroque angels and garlands of flowers. It's a gem of a place, supremely self confident and beautifully kept, full of students on bicycles, artists, musicians, outdoor cafés and cobbled streets.

Founded in the 12th century, Varaždin briefly became the capital of Croatia from 1756 to 1776, until much of the town was destroyed by fire. The result of rebuilding is a harmonious ensemble of Baroque palaces and churches, whose onion-shaped domes and towers dominate the skyline.

This is a town for gentle strolling, especially among the traffic-free streets in the centre, looking out for hidden details, from secret courtyards to coats of arms above the doors. Sooner or later you will come to the main square, **Trg Kralja Tomislava,** with its 16th-century town hall topped by an 18th-century clock tower.

Stari Grad

The one must-see sight is Stari Grad, part castle, part man-or house, reached across a drawbridge and set in its own small park, surrounded by grassy ramparts and a dried-up

A visit to Stari Grad in the quiet town of Varaždin is a must

moat. This whitewashed, red-roofed fortress, with a beautiful three-tiered courtyard in the middle, is home to the **City Museum.**

The first-floor galleries feature the town magistrate's mace and seal from 1464, as well as the original Gothic gateway to the castle. The second-floor rooms are arranged thematically to give an idea of changing aristocratic tastes in furniture, from the 16th-century Renaissance to early 20th-century Art Nouveau. Don't miss the **Kapelica Svetog Lovre** (Chapel of St Lawrence), reached along a first-floor balcony and the adjoining sacristy, set inside a round defensive tower.

A room off the courtyard features stone sculpture from Varaždin, including a 17th-century figure of the Virgin and an 18th-century pillar with carved reliefs of saints which once stood on the pilgrim route to Marija Bistrica.

Groblje
When arriving by car, look for signs to the **Groblje** (cemetery), 500m (550 yards) west of the castle, where there is a large, free, car park. Take a stroll around the cemetery, one of the most attractive in Croatia, laid out by Herman Haller in 1905.

TAKING A BREAK
Ritz (tel: 042 312 830, open Sun–Thu 9am–11pm, Fri– Sat 9am–1am, inexpensive), on the corner of the main square is a popular coffee house with a rear courtyard and a cellar lounge bar. The outdoor terrace makes a great place for people-watching during the evening *korzo*.

✚ 207 D5

Tourist Information Office
✉ Ulica Ivana Padovca 3
☎ 042 210 987; www.tourism-varazdin.hr

Stari Grad
☎ 042 212 918
🕐 Apr–Sep Tue–Sun 10–6, Oct–Mar Tue–Fri 10–5, Sat–Sun 10–1 💵 25kn

INSIDER INFO

- Look out for the **Changing of the Guard** which takes place on Saturday mornings at 11am in summer. The ceremony dates back to the 18th century and features the Purgari (Civil Guard) in their distinctive blue uniforms and bearskin hats.
- Have a look inside the **Galerija Zlati Ajngel** (Gajeva 15, tel: 042 212 702, www.ajngel.hr, Tue–Fri 6pm–8pm, Sat, Sun 10–noon). It is not just the fascinating art exhibitions that are worth seeing. The idyllic inner courtyard of a typical Varaždin townhouse is equally interesting. Varaždin is also known as the 'town of angels', as depictions of an *ajngel* are to be found on many buildings and in churches in the town, as can be seen here too.

Insider Tip

㉕ Kopački Rit

This vast, beautiful wetland reserve at the confluence of the rivers Danube and Drava is an important refuge for large numbers of nesting and migrant birds.

The Danube flood plain is one of the most significant wetland habitats in Europe, but more than 80 percent was lost during the 20th century as a result of building and over-development. The remaining area is spread over three

Picturesque sunset over the Kopački Rit wetlands

different countries (Croatia, Hungary and Serbia), with varying degrees of protection. Around 180km² (70mi²) of the Kopački Rit wetlands were declared a nature park in 1967; since 1993 it has been incorporated in the Ramsar Convention for the protection of wetlands. However, from 1991 to 1995, they were occupied by Serbian forces who laid landmines in the park. Fortunately, most of the wildlife has survived, the mines have been cleared and the area is once again safe for visitors.

Even on a short visit to Kopački Rit you will see a wide variety of fauna and flora. Much of the park is made up of willow, poplar and oak forests, home to large populations of deer, pine martens and wild boar. The rivers teem with carp, pike and catfish and the ponds of reed, sedge and waterlilies become great marshy swamps when the Danube floods in the summer.

The best introduction to the park is to take a 🚤 **boat trip** which leaves three or four times a day between March and November from a jetty close to the visitor centre. The staff will issue you with binoculars and you may see herons, cormorants and geese, or if you are lucky, even catch a glimpse of a kingfisher, a white-tailed eagle or a black stork.

Another option is to go walking in the oak forest around **Tikveš**, deep inside the park. The hunting lodge here was used by Prince Eugene of Savoy during the 18th century and later by the Yugoslavian President Tito.

TAKING A BREAK

There are two restaurants in Kopački Rit, both of which serve the local delicacy of carp roasted on a stick. The first restaurant, **Kormoran** (tel: 031 753 099), is located 4km (2.5mi) from the Podunavlje park entrance, while the second, **Tikveš** (tel: 031 752 901), can be found by the castle of the same name.

➕ 210 B3/4
☎ 031 752 320; www.kopacki-rit.com ⏱ Daily 9–5
🎟 Park entrance: 10kn. Boat trip: 100kn

INSIDER INFO

- The **main entrance** to the park is near the village of **Kopačevo**. Head north from Osijek on the main road towards Hungary and turn right at the crossroads in Bilje, then follow signs to the park. There is a large car park and a visitor office at the entrance.
- Take binoculars, good walking shoes and insect repellent as **mosquitoes can be a problem,** especially in summer.
- The park can also be explored by **bicycle.** Bikes are available to rent at the visitor centre at the entrance (10kn/hour). The nearby village of Kopačevo contains some good examples of **vernacular architecture,** with Hungarian-style houses built end-on to the road, their long galleries facing towards inner courtyards. This is part of the **Baranja,** a fertile region with close links to Hungary.

Insider Tip

㉖ Lonjsko Polje

The villages of the Lonjsko Polje Nature Park, less than 100km (62mi) from Zagreb, provide a peaceful escape from the capital, with their picturesque wooden cottages, forest walks and nesting storks in spring and summer.

The Lonjsko Polje occupies an area of around 500km² (193mi²) on the flood plains of the River Sava and its tributaries. Much of this area is made up of lowland oak forest, while the remainder is pasture meadows which turn into marshy swamps whenever the rivers rise. The flood waters attract numerous frogs and fish which in turn provide food for visiting waterfowl and white storks. Sturdy Posavina horses graze on the pasturelands and local farmers keep spotted Turopolje pigs, a rare breed which feeds off acorns and lives in the oak forests throughout the year.

Posavina horses graze on pastureland in Lonjsko Polje Nature Park

The main route through the Lonjsko Polje follows the old road from Sisak to Jasenovac, on the east bank of the Sava. The road passes through many pretty villages, but if you only have time for two, they should be **Čigoć** and **Krapje.**

🏠 Čigoć

Čigoć has been designated the first **European Stork Village** because of the large numbers of white storks that nest here in spring and can usually be seen between April and August. The imposing bird's bill-clattering can be heard during this period. Virtually every house in the village has a stork's nest on the roof. The information office issues maps of waymarked walks, including a short stroll through the forest and a two-hour walk from Čigoć across the flood dike. The Sučić Ethnographic Museum, included in the park entry ticket, has a collection of domestic and farming artefacts from the late 19th and early 20th centuries.

Krapje

Krapje, 30km (18mi) from Čigoć, is an architectural heritage village with a fine collection of traditional wooden houses and farm buildings. Several are being restored to create a new headquarters for the nature park.

The typical Posavina oak cottages are built end-on to the road, with external wooden staircases up to the living quarters on the first floor. They do not have chimneys; instead, the smoke is allowed to escape through the roof timbers and the attic is used for curing meat.

Just outside Krapje is **Krapje Đol,** Croatia's first ornithological reserve when it opened in 1963 and a haven for waterfowl, including herons, egrets and spoonbills. If you are interested in guided walks ask at the information office for further details.

Insider Tip

TAKING A BREAK

There are no restaurants in the Lonjsko Polje Nature Park, but tasty farmhouse food is available at **Rastovac** (Čigoć 44, tel: 044 715 321) and **Ravlić,** a family owned cottage in Mužilovčica (▶87).

Jasenovac concentration camp memorial, Lonjsko Polje

✠ 207 E1

Information office

✉ Čigoć 26 ☎ 044 715 115; www.pp-lonjsko-polje.hr 🕐 Daily 8–4 💰 Park: 40kn

INSIDER INFO

- Take binoculars, robust walking shoes and **insect repellent.**
- The town of **Jasenovac** was the site of the largest concentration camp in Croatia in World War II. Named after the town, it is estimated that at least 75,000 Serbs, Jews, Romany people and political opponents were murdered by the fascist Ustše government. The site is marked by the 'Stone Flower' – a giant concrete sculpture of a lotus flower by the Serbian artist Bogdan Bogdanović, a former mayor of Belgrade. In 2006 a new memorial museum opened on this site, telling the story of one of the darkest chapters in Croatian history (summer daily 10–4, winter Mon–Fri 9–4, free).

Inland Croatia

At Your Leisure

27 Samobor

When the people of Zagreb want a weekend in the country, they go to Samobor. Just 20km (12.5mi) west of the capital, this is the perfect provincial town, with handsome 19th-century townhouses around an elongated main square, dominated by an onion-domed church. The pretty **Gradna** brook runs below the church, criss-crossed by wooden bridges in an area known as **Mala Venecija** (Little Venice).

An easy climb from the middle of town leads to a ruined 13th-century castle from the days when Samobor's became a 'royal free market town' through a charter signed by King Bela IV in 1242. More serious hikers can head for **Žumberak-Samoborsko Gorje** Nature Park, a lovely region of forested hills and alpine meadows between Samobor and the Slovenian border.

Insider Tip

If all that walking works up an appetite, the cafés around the main square specialise in *samoborska kremšnita*, a flaky cream and custard cake.

➕ 206 B3

Tourist Information Office
✉ Trg Kralja Tomislava 5 ☎ 013 360 044

The birthplace of Josip Broz Tito, born in 1892, in the small village of Kumrovec

28 Kumrovec

This small village on the Slovenian border is best known as the birthplace of the Yugoslav leader Josip Broz Tito, born in 1892.

The house in which he was born was turned into a museum during his lifetime, but since his death more than 40 old buildings in the village have been reconstructed to give an idea of rural life in the Zagorje region at the end of the 19th century. The **Staro Selo** Ethnographic Museum is part of the modern village, with farmers on tractors, children on bicycles and families living in village houses alongside the exhibits. There are old farmsteads, granaries and stables, restored potters' and toymakers' studios and a reconstruction of the blacksmith's workshop once owned by Tito's parents.

A statue of Tito marks the entrance to his birthplace that now houses a display of old photos and uniforms.

The school he attended from 1900 to 1905 can also be seen. In summer there are exhibitions of rural crafts inside the various buildings and Zagorje food tasting in the old wine cellar Zagorska Klet.

➕ 206 B4

Staro Selo
☎ 049 225 830
🕐 Apr–Sep daily 9–7, Oct–Mar 9–4 💰 20kn

29 Hlebine

Set in the fertile Podravina region, close to the Hungarian border, the village of Hlebine is considered the birthplace of Croatian Naïve Art (► 56) and has been home to more than 200 painters and sculptors since the 1930s. The **Galerija Hlebine,** established in 1968, features changing displays by contemporary village artists, but also has a permanent room devoted to Ivan Generalić (1914–92), showing his development from early portraits and depictions of rural life to fantastic visions of the Eiffel Tower and Christ crucified in the winter snows of Hlebine.

✚ 207 F4

Galerija Hlebine
✉ Trg Ivana Generalića 15 ☎ 048 836 075
🕐 Tue–Fri 10–4, Sat/Sun 10–2 💰 10kn

30 Osijek

The capital of Slavonia lies on the south bank of the River Drava, roughly 30km (18mi) from both Hungary and Serbia. The heart of the city is in Gornji Grad (Upper Town), dominated by its 19th-century red-brick cathedral, but almost everything else of interest is in the 18th-century Austrian fortress of Tvrđa, 2km (1.2mi) to the east. You can get there by walking along the riverbank promenade or taking tram No 1 along Europska Avenija, a grand park-lined boulevard linking Tvrća with Gornji Grad. Osijek suffered heavy bombardment in 1991 and the damage is still visible, but Tvrđa has recovered its easy-going atmosphere, with students spilling out of the university into the cafés on the main square. The square is lined with Baroque palaces and military buildings, with a plague column dating from 1729 in the middle.

For the best views of Tvrđa, follow the riverside path and cross the elegant suspension bridge to the town beach of Copacabana, then

Detail of the plague monument in the centre of the Tvrda area, Osijek

return along the north bank and over the road bridge, from where the full extent of the fortress town is clear. *Insider Tip*

✚ 210 A3

Tourist Information Office
✉ Županijska 2
☎ 031 203 755; www.tzosijek.hr

31 Vukovar

Nowhere else in Croatia symbolises the horror of war as starkly as Vukovar. During the 1990s, the town became a byword for suffering and its name still strikes an emotional chord with every Croat. Once a prosperous market town on the west bank of the Danube, with a mixed Serbian and Croatian population and some delightful Baroque architecture, Vukovar became a battleground when it came under siege from Serbian forces for three months in 1991. At least 2,000 people died during the siege and many more were killed afterwards and buried in mass graves by the victorious Serbian paramilitaries. Th wartime atrocities still weigh heavily on the precarious balance in the population today that is made up of Croats (70%) and Serbs (30%).

Inland Croatia

EU funds have been used to rebuild much of the historical fabric that was damaged in the war. Since 2012 the Baroque Palais Eltz can also be seen again its former glory. It now houses the city museum that includes an exhibition on the history of the town with interesting archaeological artefacts from the Neolithic excavation sites in **Vučedol.** Another department is devoted to Croatian art of the 19th and 20th centuries. The archaeological museum, completed in 2012, not far from the Vučedol excavation sites, is expected to open in 2015.

A monument by the river, at the confluence of the Vuka and Danube and within sight of Serbia on the far bank, commemorates the victims of war.

Just outside town on the road to Ilok, beyond the ruined shell of the old water tower, a cemetery contains row upon row of unmarked white crosses in memory of those who were never found. Some of the atrocities committed in Vukovar are only just coming to light. This is not a place to linger, but a visit here can prompt sober reflections on the tragedy of war. The town of **Ilok** was also occupied during the war. Today, both places are making every effort to return to normality and to rebuild their towns. Some of Croatia's best white wines, such as Graševina and Traminac are now being pressed here again.

✛ 210 B3

Tourist information office & Town Museum
✉ Gradski Muzej Vukovar, Županijska 2, Strossmayerova 15
☎ 032 442 889, 032 441 270, www.turizamvukovar.hr
🕐 Mon–Fri 7–3 🖐 10kn

32 Đakovo

This central Slavonian city is notable chiefly for its imposing red-brick cathedral, built by Bishop Josip Strossmayer between 1866 and 1882.

The bishop of Đakovo was a leading figure in 19th-century Croatian history and an early advocate of the concept of Yugoslavia. With twin spires rising to 84m (275ft), the magnificent cathedral dominates the city completely. The interior is equally impressive, with frescoes, painted ceilings and a central dome. The tomb of Bishop Strossmayer lies in the cathedral crypt.

A short walk from Đakovo cathedral leads to Ulica Hrvatskih Velikana, that is a pleasant café-lined promenade. Another attraction in Đakovo is the Lipizzaner stud farm where the famous grey horses are bred.

✛ 209 F2

Tourist information office
✉ Ulica Kralja Tomislava 3
☎ 031 812 319; www.tzdjakovo.eu

Đakovo cathedral

Where to...
Stay

Prices
Expect to pay per person per night for a double room in summer:
£ under 300kn   ££ 300kn–600kn   £££ over 600kn

KOPAČKI RIT

Mala Kuća £
An alternative to staying in one of the big hotels in Osijek when visiting Kopački Rit is to try private accommodation offered by several families in the nearby village of Bilje. Set just back from the main road in a quiet residential street, Mala Kuća has two rooms in the family's house and four in a garden annexe, all with TV and shower. *Insider Tip* The friendly landlady will cook you dinner for a modest extra charge and also serves up huge breakfasts of home-made bread, eggs, bacon and potato cakes, all included in the price.
✚ 210 A4 ✉ Ritska 1, Bilje ☎ 091 244 557 7; www.smestaj-malakuca.hr

Sklepić £
Farmer Denis Sklepić has converted some of his farm buildings into comfortable bed-and-breakfast accommodation in the village of Karanac, 20km (12.5mi) north of Bilje. *Insider Tip* With log fires, antique wooden beds, traditional cooking and horse and carriage rides, a stay here gives a real taste of rural Croatia. The village lies on a wine route in the region of Baranja, close to the Hungarian border.
✚ 210 A4 ✉ Kolodvorska 58, Karanac ☎ 031 720 271; www.sklepic.hr

LONJSKO POLJE

Ravlić £
The Ravlić family welcomes visitors to their 200-year-old oak cottage, overlooking a lake on the old course of the River Sava in the village of Mužilovčica. Wooden steps lead up to a balcony and the guest room on the first floor, with its wooden beds, antique furniture and fading black-and-white photos. Geese, ducks and chickens run around the yard and the family also keep Turopolje pigs. Horse-riding, fishing and boating on the lake can all be arranged and dormitory beds are available in the old stables.
✚ 207 E1 ✉ Mužilovčica 72 ☎ 044 710 151

OSIJEK

Waldinger ££
This charming hotel occupies an Art Nouveau building facing the Croatian National Theatre. With just 16 rooms and tasteful reception areas, it is both intimate and stylish. Most of the rooms have jacuzzis and there is also a sauna and gym. The café on the ground floor hosts regular art exhibitions and has the feel of a literary salon from Austro-Hungarian Osijek. If you want something less expensive, there is a small guesthouse (£) in the garden.
✚ 210 A3 ✉ Županijska 8 ☎ 031 250 450; www.waldinger.hr

PLITVIČKA JEZERA

Jezero ££
The largest and most comfortable of the three national park hotels overlooks Lake Kozjak. There are 229 rooms, including 5 specially adapted for guests with disabilities.

Inland Croatia

Despite its get-away-from-it-all setting, there are tennis courts, a health centre, sauna, nightclub, children's playroom and business facilities. Also, all of the rooms have Internet access and satellite TV.

✚ 200 C4 ✉ Near Entrance 2
☎ 053 751 400; www.np-plitvicka-jezera.hr

SAMOBOR

Livadić ££
This 19th-century townhouse on the main square is now a delightful family-run hotel with spacious, comfortable rooms filled with antique furniture, rugs and parquet floors. The breakfast room, with its luxurious curtains and high-backed chairs, offers a daily feast of scrambled egg, cold meats, yogurt, fresh fruit and delectable pastries, while the attached café (➤ 89) is the best place to try the local cream and custard cake. The whole place oozes taste and character, transporting you back to the days of the Austro-Hungarian empire.

✚ 206 B3 ✉ Trg Kralja Tomislava 1
☎ 013 365 850; www.hotel-livadic.hr

VARAŽDIN

Maltar £
There are only five places to stay in central Varaždin and this small, friendly bed-and-breakfast above a café offers perhaps the best value, with 15 functional but comfortable rooms. There is a large car park at the back of the café and the centre of town is just a short walk away. Breakfast is served daily from 6am to noon.

✚ 207 D5 ✉ Ulica Preŝernova 1
☎ 042 311 100; www.maltar.hr

VUKOVAR

Lav ££
It is unlikely that you will want to stay long in Vukovar, but at least there is now a comfortable hotel if you should find yourself here late in the day and need to spend the night. The Hotel Lav was originally built in 1840 and has been destroyed three times in various wars, most recently during the siege of 1991. In February 2005, a new privately owned hotel opened on the ruins of the old building, with 42 rooms and four luxury apartments overlooking the River Danube.

✚ 210 B3 ✉ Strossmayerova 18
☎ 032 445 100; www.hotel-lav.hr

ZAGORJE

Lojzekova Hiža £
This traditional farmhouse near Marija Bistrica is a good example of the growing trend towards farm holidays in the Zagorje region. It has nine cosy rooms under the roof, with sloping ceilings and creaking wooden floors. Ducks and turkeys scrabble around in the yard and a stream runs through the garden. The owners make their own wine, spirits and jams. Horse riding and bicycle hire are available.

Insider Tip

✚ 206 C3 ✉ Gusakovec 116, 6km (4mi) west of Marija Bistrica
☎ 049 469 325; www.lojzekova-hiza.com

Vuglec Breg ££
A sophisticated agritourism retreat in the Zagorje vineyards. The four cottages of this hilltop hamlet 4km (2.5mi) north of Krapinske Toplice were modernised in 2006 to create charming apartments with all mod cons. The classy restaurant, Pri Kleti, prepares top-notch regional dishes and is frequently besieged at the weekend in the summer by Zagreb's movers and shakers. A wine cellar offers tastings of the estate wines and there are tennis and riding facilities for guests too.

✚ 206 C4 ✉ Sčkarićevo 151, Lepajci
☎ 049 345 015; www.vuglec-breg.hr

Where to…
Eat and Drink

Prices
Expect to pay for a starter, main course, salad and house wine or water for one:
£ under 100kn   **££** 100kn–200kn   **£££** over 200kn

KOPAČKI RIT

Kod Varge £
At rustic Kod Varge, traditional Slavonian dishes focus on carp, catfish and perch from local rivers. There is also an excellent *kulen* (salami) and spicy *ribilji paprikaš* (fish goulash).
➕ 210 A4 ✉ Ulica Kralja Zvonimira 37A, Bilje
☎ 031 750 120 🕐 Daily 9am–11pm

OSIJEK

Slavonska Kuća ££
On the edge of the fortified Tvrđa district, this folksy tavern has wooden benches and hunting and fishing trophies on the walls. The food is typically Slavonian, though one unusual offering is a starter of *riblja kobasica* (smoked fish sausage). Otherwise, it is best to stick to the classics dishes on the menu, such as *čobanec* (paprika-flavoured meat stew).
➕ 210 A3 ✉ Ulica Firingera 26
☎ 031 369 955
🕐 Mon–Sat 9am–11pm, Sun 11–5

SAMOBOR

Kavana Livadić £
Samobor is known for its *samoborska kremšnita*, a delicious cream and custard cake made of layers of flaky pastry. The cake shop attached to Hotel Livadić has the feel of a 19th-century Viennese *salon* with a modern touch.
➕ 206 B3 ✉ Trg Kralja Tomislava 1
☎ 013 365 850
🕐 Daily 8am–11pm

Samoborska Pivnica ££
Tucked in behind Hotel Livadić, this beer cellar is invitingly cosy with a low, whitewashed vaulted ceiling.
➕ 206 B3 ✉ Šmidhenova 3 ☎ 013 361 623
🕐 Daily 9am–11pm

VARAŽDIN

Palatin ££
A modern, swish café-restaurant serving Croatian and international food, including a wide range of mixed salads. Bearing in mind how dominant meat is in Croatian dishes, this is a welcome respite.
➕ 207 D5 ✉ Brače Radića 1 ☎ 042 398 300
🕐 Daily 9am–midnight

Verglec £
A delightful restaurant serving traditional fare from the Varaždin region with dishes such as wild *paprikaš* or roast pork with *mlinci*, all of impeccable quality. The portions are big enough for two.   *Insider Tip*
➕ 207 D5 ✉ Kranjčevićeva 12
☎ 042 211 131 🕐 Daily 11–11

ZAGORJE

Grešna Gorica £
This farmhouse restaurant has long wooden benches, tree trunks for tables and beautiful views across the hills to Veliki Tabor. Dishes such as venison goulash or roast pork are accompanied by home-made wine and followed by *štrukli* (cottage cheese strudel).
➕ 206 B4 ✉ Taborgradska 3, Desinić
☎ 049 343 001 🕐 Daily 10–10

Inland Croatia

Where to…
Shop

SAMOBOR

The two culinary specialities of
Samobor are *Bermet*, a herb-
flavoured vermouth and *muštarda*,
a spicy mustard, both introduced
by French troops in 1808.

You can buy them at the shop
run by the **Filipec** family, just off
the main square behind Hotel
Livadić.

Ivančic, in Plešivica, is a good
place to buy local wine.

VARAŽDIN

The pedestrianised town centre is
great for shopping, especially on
Ulica Gundulića, with shops selling
wine, leather, shoes, clothes and
souvenirs.

If you're after a silk tie, there is
a branch of **Croata** on the corner of
Trg Kralja Tomislava.

VUKOVAR

A miniature ceramic reproduction
of the Vučedol Dove (➤ 59) makes
an unusual souvenir and, since
the 1990s war, it has become a
symbol of peace.

You can buy one at the visitor
information office in the **Kopački
Rit** Nature Park. In Ilok, on the
main street in Iločki Podrumi,
some of Croatia's best white wines
are sold.

ZAGORJE

A speciality of the Zagorje region
is *licitarsko srce*, a gingerbread
heart decorated with icing which is
traditionally given as a token of
love. You can buy them in the main
square in Marija Bistrica.

Where to…
Go Out

SAMOBOR

There are **parades** with floats on
the last weekend of carnival,
when people wear masks and
fancy dress. The climax of the
festivities is a Shrove Tuesday
fireworks display.

VARAŽDIN

The streets of Varaždin come
alive every summer with artists,
musicians and costumed enter-
tainers.

On Saturday mornings at 11am
from May to September you can
see the **Changing of the Guard**
outside the town hall.

In June, a **Historical Festival**
takes place, with drama, music,
dance and medieval jousting
tournaments.

Insider Tip

The two-week **Špancirfest** street
festival (late Aug to early Sep)
features open-air concerts, acrobats
and pageants.

During the **Varaždin Baroque
Evening** events (late Sep to early
Oct), classical recitals are held in
churches and theatres.

FOLK FESTIVALS

Brodsko Kolo, held in Slavonski
Brod in mid-June, features open-
air music, dancing and a beauty
contest for the prettiest woman
in folk costume.

Đakovački Vezovi (Đakovo
Embroidery), in Đakovo, usually
during the first weekend
in July, is another big event,
with *tamburica* (Slavonian mandolin) music, Lipizzaner horses
and traditional wedding
carriages.

Istria and Beyond

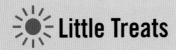 **Little Treats**

Out and about with the locals
Take a boat trip from **Rovinjer Batana Museum**
(► 102) that includes wine and sardines in
a traditional tavern.

Sipping on the seaside
The Safari Bar at the furthermost point
of **Kamenjak peninsula** (► 106) has second-
hand furnishings found elsewhere and
straw mats – totally hip!

Pub crawl
The bars in the **Trsat** district of Rijeka
(► 107) are packed with students until
the early hours of the morning.

Getting Your Bearings

Istria (Istra in Croatian) is the most cosmopolitan region of Croatia. Being the most northerly peninsula on the Adriatic it has absorbed the influences of nearby Italy, both in its language and its cuisine. Its cultural heritage – from the Roman and Byzantine eras to its imperial Austro-Hungarian past – has turned this wealthy and self-confident region into an attraction for millions of visitors from all over Europe.

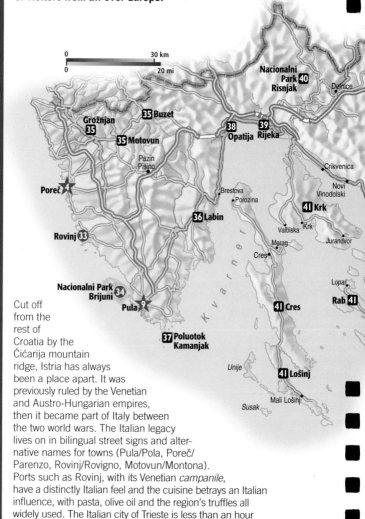

Cut off from the rest of Croatia by the Ćićarija mountain ridge, Istria has always been a place apart. It was previously ruled by the Venetian and Austro-Hungarian empires, then it became part of Italy between the two world wars. The Italian legacy lives on in bilingual street signs and alternative names for towns (Pula/Pola, Poreč/Parenzo, Rovinj/Rovigno, Motovun/Montona). Ports such as Rovinj, with its Venetian *campanile*, have a distinctly Italian feel and the cuisine betrays an Italian influence, with pasta, olive oil and the region's truffles all widely used. The Italian city of Trieste is less than an hour away and Venice a short trip by catamaran.

Not surprisingly, given its proximity to central Europe, Istria is where tourism has made the greatest impact. Coastal towns such as Poreč, Rovinj and Pula reverberate with Italian and German accents and there is a real buzz on summer evenings as people stroll along the promenades. Just inland is a different Istria – an Istria of vineyards, olive groves, oak woods and hilltop towns. To the south, Kvarner bay separates Istria from Dalmatia, with Croatia's two largest islands, Krk and Cres, sheltering beneath the Gorski Kotar and Velebit mountains.

A cobbled street in Rovinj is the perfect location for an art gallery

Perfect Days in...

Three Perfect Days

If you're not quite sure where to begin your trip, this itinerary recommends a practical and enjoyable three-day tour of the best of both coastal and inland Istria. For more information see the main entries (▶ 96).

Day 1

Morning

Take a walk around the Old Town of ⭐**Poreč** and admire the beautiful mosaics and frescoes (left) in the **Basilica of Euphrasius.**

Lunch

Follow the coast road south from Poreč to Vrsar and head inland following the bank of the Limski Kanal (▶ 101). The village of Flengi has several roadside restaurants specialising in spit-roast pork. Alternatively, beyond the hamlet of Kloštar, a side road leads down to a bay where several restaurants sell local oysters and mussels.

Afternoon and evening

Return to the coast at ❸❸ **Rovinj** (▶ 100) and explore the Old Town. Climb up to the Church of St Euphemia to watch the sun set before enjoying a drink at one of the waterside bars. Take your pick of the restaurants (top right) and finish off with an ice-cream on the promenade.

Nacionalni Park Risnjak ❹❶

Grožnjan ❸❺ ❸❺ Buzet Opatija ❸❽ ❸❾

❸❺ Motovun Rijeka

Poreč ⭐

❸❻ Labin ❹❶ Krk

Rovinj ❸❸

Nacionalni park Brijuni ❸❹ Pula Rab ❹❶

⭐ ❹❶ Cres

❸❼ Poluotok Kamanjak

❹❶ Lošinj

Day 2

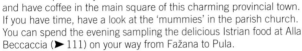

Morning
Make an early start to drive down to Fažana, the starting point for the boat trip to 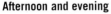 **34 Nacionalni Park Brijuni** (➤ 103). You can spend several hours exploring Veli Brijun on a guided tour on foot and on the miniature road train which tours the safari park.

Afternoon and evening
Returning to Fažana, make the short trip to Vodnjan and have coffee in the main square of this charming provincial town. If you have time, have a look at the 'mummies' in the parish church. You can spend the evening sampling the delicious Istrian food at Alla Beccaccia (➤ 111) on your way from Fažana to Pula.

Day 3

Morning
Head into the Old Town in bustling ★ **Pula** (➤ 98) to see the Roman amphitheatre (below), then climb to the hilltop fortress for wonderful views, before relaxing with a drink on the old Roman forum.

Afternoon
Take the fast road from Pula to Pazin to begin a tour of Istria's hilltop towns **35 Motovun and Buzet** (➤ 105). Restaurants specialise in truffle dishes, so look forward to a hearty late lunch.

Evening
Watch the sun set from the church terrace in the nearby hill town of **Grožnjan** (➤ 105), then have a drink in the shade of the arches of the Venetian loggia. Afterwards, return to Motovun for dinner – the town is much quieter once the day-trippers have left and it is a peaceful and atmospheric place to spend a night.

Poreč

The most popular tourist centre in Croatia has a charming Old Town, with the most exquisite works of art in the whole country hidden down tiny alleyways. The mosaics in the Euphrasian Basilica, for example, are among the finest anywhere in Europe.

The first sight of Poreč is not promising. Between the 1960s and 1980s, it spearheaded tourism in Croatia and the town became almost completely engulfed by the tourist complexes of Lanterna to the north and Plava Laguna and Zelena Laguna to the south. The Poreč Riviera has beds to <accommodate 100,000 visitors.

Somehow, in the middle of all this, the Old Town survives intact, on a fortified peninsula where the Romans built their settlement of Parentium. The original Roman grid plan still exists, right down to the names of the intersecting north–south and east–west main streets, Cardo Maximus and Decumanus. Not far from the junction of these two streets is a magnificent example of early Christian architecture, designated a UNESCO World Heritage Site in 1997.

The Euphrasian Basilica

You enter the basilica complex through the atrium, a delightful arcaded courtyard. On your left is the **octagonal baptistry,** with a deep font in the middle, and the entrance

In the Euphrasian Basilica in Poreč the eye is automatically drawn to the magnificent mosaics

to the 16th-century **bell tower** that can be climbed for a view over the rooftops.

On the right as you enter the courtyard is the undoubted highlight of the complex, the **basilica** itself. It was built between 535 and 550 AD by Bishop Euphrasius, on the site of an earlier church dedicated to St Maurus, a 3rd-century martyr and the first bishop of Poreč.

The long central **nave,** with its Greek marble columns and arches, leads the eye towards the apse, richly adorned with Byzantine mosaics encrusted with gold leaf and mother-of-pearl. The upper panel of the principle mosaic depicts Christ, the Light of the World, with his apostles on either side. Beneath this is an arch with the Lamb of God at the centre. The semi-dome in the apse features a Virgin and Child, surrounded by saints and angels. To the left of the Virgin are St Maurus next to an angel and Bishop Euphrasius holding a model of the church. A baldachin from the 13th-century, also beautifully decorated with mosaics, dominates the chancel.

TAKING A BREAK

There are numerous cafés on Decumanus and the promenade along the shore Obala Maršala Tita. A good place for lunch is **Pizzeria Nono,** near the tourist information office (Zagrebačka 4, tel: 052 453 088).

✚ 198 A4

Basilica
✉ Eufrazijeva
🕑 Basilica, bell-tower and museum mid-Jun–Aug Mon–Sat 9.30am–10pm, May–mid-Jun, Sep until 8pm, Mar, Apr, Oct until 7pm, winter until c. 4pm
💶 bell-tower and museum 30kn, basilica free

Tourist Information Office
✉ Zagrebačka 9
☎ 052 451 293; www.to-porec.comw

INSIDER INFO

- **Classical concerts** are held in summer (generally on Fridays).
- In summer, you can take a water-taxi to the wooded island of **Sveti Nikola,** a lovely retreat where the first public beach in Poreč was opened in 1895.
- Look carefully on the right-hand side of the apse in the Euphrasian Basilica for the **mosaic of the Visitation** that shows a servant furtively drawing back the curtain and listening in on Mary's conversation with her cousin Elizabeth.

Insider Tip

In more depth: the **bishop's palace,** entered from the atrium in the basilica, contains a museum of religious art. In the garden are the remains of a 4th-century mosaic floor from the original Church of St Maurus that features a fish, the symbol and distinguishing mark used by early Christians who frequently had to practice their faith in secret.

 # Pula

The largest town in Istria is an appealing mixture of bustling port, sprawling holiday resort and historic Roman settlement, dominated by a magnificently preserved Roman amphitheatre.

Once the most important Roman city in Istria and a major naval base for the Habsburgs, Pula has become a magnet for tourists thanks to its well-preserved Old Town. Most holiday complexes are to the south of Pula on the Punta Verudela peninsula.

The Roman amphitheatre in Pula is made from Istrian limestone

🚻 The Arena

Begun around 30 BC during the reign of Emperor Augustus and completed during the 1st century, this is the sixth-largest **Roman amphitheatre** in the world. It was built of Istrian limestone and given an elliptical shape, some 130m (425ft) across and 100m (330ft) wide. It gained its present appearance some 70 years later under Emperor Vespasian who also commissioned the Colosseum in Rome. The lower level without any openings carries two rows of arches above on the side facing the sea; on the side into the slope it has just one row of arches. The upper storey comprises a row of square window openings. In its time, it held 30,000 spectators for gladiatorial contests. Even today, it is still an atmospheric place which makes the Arena so popular among children too.

During the 16th century there were plans to transport the arena stone by stone to Venice to be rebuilt there, but fortunately it has survived *in situ*. Not only the sheer scale is impressive, the museum on viniculture and olive oil production in Istria, set up on the lower level, is also worth visiting.

The Arch of Sergi dominates the Trg Portara today

Other Roman sights

Two other interesting buildings from the Roman period are easy to reach on foot from here: The **Temple of Augustus** was completed in 14AD and dedicated to the first Roman emperor. The temple, with its tall Corinthian columns, stands on the edge of the old Roman forum. During the summer, its collection of Roman sculpture is open to visitors. The largest square in the town today is to be found on the site of the Ancient Roman forum. The **Arch of Sergi,** also known as Zlatna Vrata (Golden Gate), is a triumphal arch erected by a wealthy family in the 1st century BC to honour three brothers who had fought in the battle of Actium in 31 BC.

TAKING A BREAK

Cvajner Caffe (Forum 2) occupies a prime spot on the main square. Take a table outside or opt for the comfy sofas, modern works of art and 16th-century frescoes inside.

➕ 198 B2

Tourist Information Office
✉ Forum 3 ☎ 052 212 987; www.pulainfo.hr

Arena
✉ Ulica Flavijevska ☎ 052 219 028 🕐 Jul/Aug 8am–midnight, May, Jun and Sep until 9pm, Apr until 8pm, Oct 9–7, Nov–Mar 9–5 💶 40kn

Temple of Augustus
✉ Forum 🕐 Mid-May–Jun Mon–Fri 9–9, Jul, Aug 9am–10pm, Sep 9–8, Sep–mid-May Sat, Sun 9–3 💶 10kn

INSIDER INFO

- Large shows and events are held in the Roman arena, such as the 🔟 **Days of Antiquity – Pula Superiorum** at the beginning of June, when gladiators and Roman soldiers appear in the amphitheatre (www.pulasuperiorum.com). But look out for **jazz and classical concerts** in summer in the courtyard of the castle or in the 'Small Roman Theatre' behind the Archaeological Museum.
- Climb to the Venetian **Kaštel,** a star-shaped fortress at the summit of the Old Town. The views from the ramparts and the old watchtower are magnificent.
- A visit to the 🔟 **aquarium** in the former imperial Verudela Fort is fun for the whole family. The pools, designed to provide a habitat suited to each species, are home to aquatic animals from the Adriatic Sea as well as from tropical waters. The affiliated research institute cares for threatened turtles that are being bred there before being released into the wild (June–Aug 9am–10pm, April, May, Sep 10–6, Oct–March 10–4, 60kn).
- Hidden behind the car park close to the Forum is a perfectly preserved **2nd-century Roman floor mosaic** depicting the Punishment of Dirce legend in which the children of Zeus tie their step-mother to the horns of a bull.

Insider Tip

Insider Tip

Istria and Beyond

㉝ Rovinj

Rovinj, with its brightly painted houses reflected in the water, huddled onto a steep-sided peninsula crowned by a Venetian-style church, is the most attractive town in Istria and one of the prettiest spots on the entire Croatian coast.

Even if the hordes of tourists who squeeze their way through the Old Town in the summer might make you come to a different conclusion, Rovinj has in fact managed to preserve a balance between being a historic town, a fishing port and a modern tourist resort more than any-where else in Istria. Up until the beginning of the 20th century, cigarettes were still being produced in a factory right on the harbourside. This is the most Italian place in Croatia with a sizeable Italian-speaking population.

Rovinj is one of the most charming spots on the coast

The Old Town

The oldest part of Rovinj was built on an island which was only joined to the mainland in 1763. The obvious approach is from **Trg Maršala Tita,** the large open square in front of the harbour. A Baroque 17th-century palace off the square is home to the **Rovinj Heritage Museum,** with archaeological displays, a gallery of Old Masters and contemporary art exhibitions. To get to the museum, walk through the **Balbi Arch** just off the square which was erected in 1680 and crowned by the winged lion of St Mark, the symbol of Venice.

Passing under the arch you enter the Old Town, a warren of narrow, steep, cobbled streets with hidden courtyards. More recently, Rovinj has become something of an artists' colony and the main street, **Grisia,** is lined with art galleries

and artists selling their work – particularly on the second Sunday in August when an open-air competition is held. The streets to either side of Grisia, with washing hanging from balconies, are very atmospheric.

The Church

Whichever route you take you will eventually arrive at the Baroque **Church of St Euphemia** which dominates the Old Town. The **bell tower,** over 60m (195ft) tall, was built in 1677 and modelled on the *campanile* of St Mark's in Venice. The rest of the church was built in the 18th century, though the façade is a 19th-century addition.

The church is dedicated to St Euphemia, a 3rd-century Christian from Asia Minor who was martyred during the reign of Diocletian and her body thrown to the lions. Five centuries after her death, the marble sarcophagus containing her body is said to have disappeared from Constantinople and washed up in Rovinj in 800AD. Since that time, the people of Rovinj have treated Euphemia as their patron saint and celebrate her feast day on 16 September.

The sarcophagus lies in an aisle to the right of the main altar and a copper statue of St Euphemia next the wheel on which she was tortured acts as a weather-vane on top of the bell tower. You can climb the 200 steep and rickety steps inside the tower for fantastic, panoramic views of Rovinj.

Explore the lanes and alleyways in Rovinj, lined with art shops

Beaches and islands

Locals gather in summer on the rocks beneath the church where there are several concrete platforms for sunbathing.

LIMSKI KANAL

The west coast of Istria is cut in two by the **Limski Kanal**, a narrow, 10km (6mi)-long, fiord-like estuary that lies dramatically between thickly wooded slopes and limestone cliffs. **Boat tours** of the Limski Kanal are offered from the quay in Poreč, Vrsar and Rovinj in summer and usually include a visit to a cave once used by pirates and hermits.

A better option is to follow the coastal promenade south from the marina into **Zlatni Rt forest park**, laid out by Baron Hütterodt between 1890 and 1910.

From the cape, there are good views to **Crveni Otok** (Red Island), the largest of Rovinj's archipelago which is actually two islets connected by a causeway. The bigger island is home to Hotel Istra (▶ 111), while the smaller one is virtually undeveloped and has several nudist beaches. Boats to Crveni Otok depart regularly in summer from the main town harbour and the Delfin jetty by the marina. There are also boats to **Svetia Katarina**, an island hotel just offshore from Rovinj.

A lovely close to a day on holiday: an evening meal in one of the restaurants in the Old Town of Rovinj

TAKING A BREAK

Take your pick of the many cafés and restaurants around the waterfront. **Baccus**, just off the main square at Via Carrera 5, has Istrian wines by the glass and sells truffles and olive oil.

✚ 198 A3

Museum
✉ Trg Maršala Tita 11 ☎ 052 816 720 🕓 Summer Tue–Fri 9–2, 7pm–10pm, Sat, Sun 10–2, 7pm–10pm, winter Tue–Sat 10–1 💵 15kn

Tourist Information Office
✉ Obala Pina Budicina 12 ☎ 052 811 566; www.tzgrovinj.hr

INSIDER INFO

Insider Tip

- **Watch the sunset** from the church terrace or from Valentino (Ulica Svetog Križa 28), a trendy cocktail bar with cushions, positioned so that you can almost dip your toes in the sea.
- With a little bit of luck you may see some *batana* boats on the harbour mole. If not, you can find out more about the history of these traditional fishing vessels and about fishing in general in the **Eko-muzej Batana**. Events organised by the museum – including a trip on a batana or an evening in the typical tavern **Spacio Matika** are especially good (Ob. P. Budićina 2; www.batana.org, summer daily 10–3, 6–10, winter Tue–Sun 10–1, 3–5, 10kn).

34 Nacionalni Park Brijuni

Roman emperors, Austrian princes and Communist heads of state have all enjoyed relaxing on these islands just off the Istrian coast that offer a superb blend of scenic beauty and historical sites.

The Brijuni National Park is an **archipelago** of 14 islands, 3km (2mi) offshore from the fishing port of Fažana. Only the two largest islands, **Veli Brijun** and **Mali Brijun**, can be visited. Two thousand years ago, Veli Brijun was a summer refuge for wealthy Romans – the remains of a 1st-century Roman villa can be seen in Verige Bay. Among other sights are a **Byzantine fortress** on the west coast and a 15th-century **Venetian church** with frescoes and inscriptions in Glagolitic script (➤ 179).

Veli Brijun in the 20th century

In 1893 the islands were bought by the Austrian industrialist Paul Kupelwieser. He employed the Nobel prize-winning bacteriologist Robert Koch to rid the islands of malaria, then he created a resort for fashionable European socialites. The Austrian Archduke Franz Ferdinand and the author Thomas Mann were among guests to visit Brijuni and enjoy its hotels, casino, polo club, golf course and heated sea-water pool.

In 1947, Tito chose **Brijuni** as his summer retreat and for the rest of his life he spent up to six months of the year here, entertaining world leaders from Fidel Castro of Cuba to Queen Elizabeth II. In all, some 90 heads of state visited Brijuni, including President Nehru of India and President Nasser of Egypt, who signed the founding pact of the Non-Aligned Movement here in 1956. Since

Bird's-eye view of Brijuni National Park

Zebras also roam the safari park on Veli Brijun

Tito's death, the islands have continued to be used by Croatian leaders. It was here in 1995 that President Tuđman held a controversial meeting with his generals on the eve of Operation Storm, to capture Serbian Krajina.

Trips and tours

You can visit **Veli Brijun** on a national park boat trip from Fažana which run several times a day in summer and upon request in winter; advance booking is essential. In summer, there are also organised excursions from Pula and Rovinj. The cost includes a three-hour guided tour by miniature train, crossing open parkland with fallow deer on your way to the 🏆 **safari park** which is home to animals bred from those given to Tito by world leaders.

Insider Tip

The tour also includes a visit to the **Natural History Museum**. Upstairs, the 'Tito on Brijuni' exhibition has photos of Tito with his many visitors, relaxing in his orchards and wine cellar and hunting in his private game reserve. Tito's official residence, the Bijela Vila (White Villa), can be glimpsed behind high hedges and walls on the west coast and is still protected by security guards.

TAKING A BREAK

There is a café near the harbour at **Veli Brijun** and restaurants in various hotels.

✚ 198 A3

National Park Boat Trips
✉ Brijunska 10, Fažana ☎ 052 525 882; www.brijuni.hr 🕐 um 200kn

INSIDER INFO

Insider Tip

- Guests staying at hotels on Veli Brijun can rent bicycles and electric golf buggies to explore the island on their own.
- There is also a daily excursion from Fažana in summer to **Mali Brijun** which includes a visit to an Austro-Hungarian fortress, swimming and a picnic.

At Your Leisure

The fortified town of Buzet is the largest of the hill towns of Istria

35 Motovun, Buzet and Grožnjan

Inland Istria, with its olive groves, vineyards, rolling green hills and fortified hilltop towns, is often compared to the Italian region of Tuscany. Many villages have been more or less deserted, but those seeking an alternative lifestyle, artists and tourism have ultimately ensured that life is returning.

Motovun, perched 277m (906ft) above the **Mirna valley** is surrounded by oak forests and vineyards producing Malvazija and Teran wines. You enter Motovun through the **Old Town gate**, its walls lined with Roman inscriptions and Venetian stone lions; turn left next to the loggia to arrive at the elongated main square, dominated by its 13th-century *campanile*. Note the old well in the square and the relief of the winged lion of St Mark, dating from 1322. From here you can walk around the **medieval ramparts** that offer superb views. Recently, Motovun has become increasingly fashionable, especially during the annual film festival in late July. The largest of the hill towns, high above the River Mirna, is **Buzet**; from here it is a short trip to **Glagolitic Alley** (➤ 179) and the miniature hill town of **Hum**. In autumn you may see farmers with dogs looking for truffles in the oak woods around both towns.

Another town which has been given a new lease of life is **Grožnjan**. It was virtually abandoned in the 1960s until it was declared a 'town of artists' and old, stone cottages were rented out to painters and musicians. The cobbled streets and squares are ideal for a stroll, with **art galleries** and an **international summer school** of young musicians bringing life and atmosphere back to the town.

➕ 198 A4, B4, B5

Tourist Information Office
✉ Trg Andrea Antico 1, Motovun
☎ 052 681 642; www.tz-motovun.hr

36 Labin

This medieval hill town above the east Istrian coast makes a delightful place to while away a couple of hours. It has a laid-back atmos-

Rijeka: the Korzo forms the very heart of the town

phere, art galleries and studios and Renaissance and Baroque palaces lining the cobbled streets. From the main square, **Titov Trg**, pass through the town gate and climb the steps to reach the **Church of the Virgin Mary**, notable for the Venetian winged lion on the façade.

The nearby **Lazzarini Palace** houses the **Labin National Museum** whose most interesting exhibit, a reconstruction of a coal mine, commemorates the town's mining history. Afterwards, you can walk around the town walls for views of **Rabac**, a small fishing village 4km (2.5mi) below **Labin**, where pebble coves and beaches attract visitors.
➕ 198 C3

Insider Tip

Tourist Information Office
✉ Aldo Negri 20 ☎ 052 855 560,
www.rabac-labin.com

National Museum
🕐 In summer Mon–Fri 10–1, 5pm–7pm, Sat/
Sun 10–1, in winter Mon–Fri 10–3 💶 15kn

37 👥 Poluotok Kamenjak

The peninsula is a conservation area some 10km (6.2mi) long and between 400m and 1.5km (0.25mi–1mi) wide and forms the southern-most tip of Istria. Campsites and holiday villages line the coast at the start near the village of Premantura. However, once you pass the toll gate (fee for cars: 25kn) a natural landscape opens up before you, best explored by bike or on foot, with cliffs up to 12m (39ft) high, lonely pebbly beaches and a fascinating wealth of orchids. Right at the beginning of the peninsula petrified dinosaur footprints can be seen in a bay and a short nature trail gives you all sorts of information about dinosaur finds in the area. A visit to the **Safari Bar** at the end of the peninsula, with furniture made of driftwood and other objects found by chance, is a must.

Cycling around the peninsula is easy for children too. If they get tired, a leap into the water soon wakes them up again. Bikes can be hired at the Windsurfing Center Premantura (www.windsurfing.hr), for example; mountainbikes are best.

🏛 198 B2 ✉ Centar 223, Medulin ☎ 052 577 147; www.medulinriviera.info

🔢 Opatija

Opatija is sheltered by the peak **Učka** from the cold *bora* wind. Its unique microclimate on the shores of **Kvarner Bay** made it a popular winter resort for the Habsburg aristocracy whose *belle époque* villas and hotels still stand on the seafront today, harbouring the spirit of an earlier age. Royal families, dukes and playwrights such as Anton Chekhov (1860–1904) all stayed here; the dancer Isadora Duncan (1877–1927) was inspired to create her most famous movement by the fluttering of a tree outside her window.

The finest remnant of the Habsburg era is **Villa Angiolina**, set in its own park next to the Kvarner Hotel (▶ 110). A 12km (7.5 mile) seafront promenade, the **Lungomare** (officially Šetalište Franz Josef I), connects **Opatija** with **Volosko north and Lovran south** and makes an equally enchanting walk by day or night, with palm and cypress trees, lush gardens, rocky coves and old-fashioned lamps.

🏛 198 C4

Tourist Information Office
✉ Maršala Tita 101 ☎ 051 271 310; www.opatija-tourism.hr

🔢 Rijeka

Croatia's biggest port is badly marred on the outskirts by industry. The old, ochre-coloured, Habsburg-era buildings right on the waterfront are adorned with reliefs and sculptures on nautical themes.

Just behind the harbour, the **Korzo** is the main shopping street and focus of street life. An arch beneath the clock tower leads to

Leska nature trail in Nationalpark Risnjak is a delight

the oldest part of Rijeka that is centred on the Church of St Vitus. Climb the long flight of steps from the Rječina River or take bus no. 1 to the pilgrimage church of **Trsat**, where legend has it that angels transported the house of the Virgin Mary to this spot in 1291. There are good views over the **Rječima gorge** from nearby Trsat Castle (summer daily 9–8, winter 9–5), restored in the 19th century as a romantic folly. The castle and the church lie at the heart of a lively bar scene.

🏛 199 D4

Tourist Information Office
✉ Korzo 33 ☎ 051 335 882, www.visitrijeka.eu

🔢 Nacionalni Park Risnjak

When the heat of the coast gets too much, escape to this national park inland from Rijeka, with its cool beech and fir forests among the mountains of Gorski Kotar. Bears, wolves and lynx inhabit these forests, though you

The islands around Kvarner Bay as seen from mainland Croatia

are unlikely to see any of them. The park office is in the village of **Crni Lug**; from here you can follow the Leska Trail, a well-marked 4km (2.5 mile) circuit which gives a gentle introduction to the landscapes of this region. A tougher hike leads to the summit of **Veliki Risnjak** (1528m/5013ft).

Insider Tip

✚ 199 E5 ✉ Crni Lug ☎ 051 836 133, http://risnjak.hr 🎫 Free

⁴¹ Cres, Lošinj, Krk, Rab

The wide **Kvarner Gulf** separates Istria to the north from the Dalmatian coast to the south. Although not as attractive as some of the islands further south, those in Kvarner bay offer Roman and Venetian history, pretty harbourside towns and some of Croatia's best beaches. Each of the three main islands can be reached by ferry or a bridge from the mainland, but they can also be combined on an **island-hopping tour**, with ferries that link Krk to Cres and Rab in summer.

Cres

This long, narrow island, 65km (40mi) from north to south, is actually a continuation of the partially submerged **Učka mountain range**.

It is reached by regular ferries from **Brestova** in Istria and from **Valbiska** on Krk. The northern part of the island is forested and green, while the south is increasingly rocky and used mainly for sheep pastures.

The capital of the island, **Cres**, sits in a pretty bay sheltered by green hills and makes a pleasant place to stroll, with its Venetian loggia, clock tower, town gates and Renaissance palaces. **Osor**, on the south coast, is the oldest settlement on the island and today it has the character of an open-air museum, with its stone houses, cobbled streets and 15th-century cathedral. From Osor, a swing bridge connects Cres to the nearby island of Lošinj.

Lošinj

A bridge connects Osor with the island of Lošinj. Unlike austere Cres, green Lošinj has a rich vegetation and wonderfully smelling woods. **Mali Lošinj**, the main centre on the island, is a lively little harbour town with proud captains' houses and a wide choice of culinary fare. **Veli Lošinj** on the other hand is much quieter. The elegant villas lining the almost circular **Čikat Bay**, that have since been converted into hotels, are a reminder of imperial times when people came here to take the sea air.

Krk

Croatia's largest island is reached by a toll bridge at **Kraljevica**, on the coast road south of Rijeka. With its easy access to central Europe and Rijeka airport, **Krk** is a popular tourist destination. The northwest coast is dominated by package-holiday resorts at **Omišalj**, **Njivice** and **Malinska**.

The capital, Krk, was the old **Roman city of Curicum**. Traces of the Roman walls survive, along with a Romanesque cathedral and the 12th-century Church of St Quirinus, their shared bell tower topped by a distinctive onion dome. **Baška**, at the southern tip of the island, has a 2km (1.2-mile) beach of sand and pebbles, with views of the **Velebit mountain range** across the water. The beach gets crowded in summer, but you can always take a water-taxi to one of the nearby bays. Just inland from Baška, in the church at Jurandvor, is a copy of the Baška Tablet, an 11th-century stone containing the earliest known example of the Glagolitic script (➤ 179). The original is in Zagreb.

Rab

Rab is the most attractive of the Kvarner islands. The east coast, facing the mainland, is harsh and barren, battered by the *bora* wind, but the west coast is green and dotted with sheltered bays and coves. There are sandy beaches at **Lopar, San Marino** and **Kampor**, but the real highlight of the island is **Rab Town**, set on a peninsula beside its harbour. Open squares on the waterfront lead into the Old Town, a warren of narrow lanes intersected by three parallel streets – **Donja Ulica** (Lower Street), **Srednja Ulica** (Middle Street) and **Gornja Ulica** (Upper Street). The distinctive feature of Rab, seen from the water, is the row of bell towers silhouetted against the sky-line; you can see them all from the only remaining section of the medieval walls. You can also climb the tallest of the *campanile* for views over the rooftops.

There is good swimming from the seafront promenade beneath **Komrčar Park**, or you can take a taxi-boat to **Kandarola** on the Frkanj peninsula, a nudist beach popularised by the British king Eduard VIII (➤ 16). Ferries run to Rab throughout the year from Jablanac, 100km (62mi) south of Rijeka.

Cres
🔛 198 C2
Tourist Information Office
✉ Cons 10, Cres town ☎ 051 571 535, www.tzg-cres.hr

Lošinj
🔛 199 D1
Tourist Information Office
✉ Riva lošinjskih kapetana 29, Mali Lošinj
☎ 051 231 884; www.tz-malilosinj.hr

Krk
🔛 199 E3
Tourist Information Office
✉ Obala hrvatske mornarice, Krk
☎ 051 220 226; www.tz-krk.hr

Rab
🔛 199 D2
Tourist Information Office
✉ Trg Municipium Arba 8, Rab
☎ 051 724 064; www.tzg-rab.hr

Above the rooftops of Rab

Where to…
Stay

Prices
Expect to pay per person per night for a double room in summer:
£ under 300kn   **££** 300kn–600kn   **£££** over 600kn

BRIJUNI ISLANDS

Neptun-Istra £££
Although it no longer has the cachet it enjoyed in the early 20th century, Veli Brijun still attracts the rich and famous. This somewhat overpriced hotel right on the quay has lots of rooms and suites and a still has a Socialist air about it. The price includes unlimited boat trips to and from the mainland. You can rent bicycles, boats and horses and discounts at the nearby golf course are available for hotel guests.
✚ 198 A3 ✉ Veli Brijun ☎ 052 525 807; www.brijuni.hr

MOTOVUN, BUZET & GROŽNJAN

Kaštel ££
Set in an 18th-century townhouse on the main square of Motovun, Kaštel succeeds in combining traditional and modern styles. All the rooms are brightly decorated and there is an art gallery, a peaceful garden and a pool. *Insider Tip* From the rooftop terrace there are views across the ramparts to the Mirna valley. The restaurant specialises in truffle dishes.
✚ 198 B4 ✉ Trg Andrea Antico 7, Motovun ☎ 052 681 607; www.hotel-kastel-motovun.hr

OPATIJA

Kvarner ££
The *grande dame* of Opatija's hotels may have lost a little of its sparkle since it opened its doors in 1884, but it is still the only place to stay if you want to capture the faded elegance of this Habsburg-era resort. The cream-coloured Classicist façade adorned with trumpeting angels harks back to a bygone age and the flower-filled gardens tumble down to the sea. *Insider Tip* Facilities include heated pools.
✚ 198 C4 ✉ Ulica Tomašića 1–4 ☎ 051 710 444; www.remisens.com

Mozart £££
Relive the atmosphere of *belle époque* Opatija at this stylish boutique hotel, with its striking pink façade, Art Nouveau lobby and 26 rooms, most with balconies overlooking the sea. Despite being fitted with all modern comforts, the five-star hotel consciously imitates the Habsburg era, with staff in period costume, a Viennese-style coffee house, a pianist playing Mozart and rooms decorated in the Austro-Hungarian style.
✚ 198 C4 ✉ Maršala Tita 138 ☎ 051 718 260; www.hotel-mozart.hr

POREČ

Fortuna ££
Insider Tip This large modern hotel on the wooded island of Sveti Nikola is a 5-minute boat ride from Poreč on the hotel's hourly shuttle boats. It faces towards the harbour in Poreč and most rooms have balconies with sea views. Among the facilities are outdoor pools, tennis courts, watersports, a place to sunbathe and swim on the rocky coastline that belongs to the hotel, a children's playground and in-house entertainment every evening.

The hotel also rents out apartments in Isabella Castle, a 19th-century villa on the island. Cars cannot be taken to the island, but there is a secure car park near the harbour.

➕ 198 A4 ✉ Otok Sveti Nikola
☎ 052 406 000; www.valamar.com 🕐 Apr–Oct

Grand Hotel Palazzo £££

Built in 1910, the hotel has an incomparably beautiful location at the tip of the peninsula in the Old Town with uninterrupted sea views. The flair of the olden days, modern facilities, quiet and yet centrally situated. The restaurant serves Croatian food with an international touch.

➕ 198 A4 ✉ Obala Maršala Tita 24
☎ 052 858 800, http://hotel-palazzo.hr

PULA

Alla Beccaccia ££

This appealing *agriturismo* guest-house half way between Fažana and Pula has comfortable rooms with modern furnishings, each with its own terrace. Small pool and excellent restaurant.

➕ 198 B2 ✉ Pineta 25, Valbandon, Fažana
☎ 052 520 753 0; www.beccaccia.hr

Scaletta ££

This small, charming hotel on the road to the amphitheatre is among the most attractive in Pula. There are only 12 quietly stylish rooms in this old townhouse, all decorated in warm pastel shades, with private bathrooms and air-conditioning. Reservation essential. The adjacent restaurant is one of the best in Pula.

➕ 198 B2 ✉ Ulica Flavijevska 26
☎ 052 541 025; www.hotel-scaletta.com

ROVINJ

Adriatic ££

The oldest hotel in Rovinj, opened in 1912, has a prime position on the waterfront in a corner of Trg Maršala Tita main square. It is worth paying extra for a room with a sea view, looking out beyond the harbour to the island of Sveti Katarina. The rooms are comfortable and spacious and the hotel has retained some of the original charm from the age of the Danube monarchy, particularly in its Viennese-style café. It is a good place to stay if you want to be at the heart of the action, with restaurants and bars on the promenade only a few yards away.

➕ 198 A3 ✉ Obala Pina Budicina
☎ 052 800 250; www.maistra.hr

Istra ££

Although it is something of an eyesore on the beautiful island of Crveni Otok, this large modern hotel is a good place to stay if you want a relaxing beach holiday within easy reach of Rovinj. The 352 rooms, including some family rooms, are simply furnished but comfortable. There is swimming from the rocky shore and several nudist beaches on a nearby islet, reached across a causeway. You can rent a canoe or motorboat, go windsurfing, swim in the pool, play tennis, take your kids to the playground, or eat in various restaurants and bars. And whenever you tire of the island, you can hop on the shuttle boat to Rovinj which operates hourly throughout the summer until midnight.

➕ 198 A3 ✉ Crveni Otok
☎ 052 802 500; www.maistra.hr 🕐 Apr–Oct

🏨 Lone £££

If you always wanted to spend the night in a perfect design hotel, then this is the place for you! Lone is the best hotel in Rovinj and guests who stay in one of the 236 totally trendy rooms are spoilt with a choice of several restaurants and a fantastic spa area and beach. And it is exceptionally child-friendly too.

➕ 198 A3 ✉ Luje Adamovića 31,
☎ 052 800 250; www.lonehotel.com

Where to...
Eat and Drink

Prices
Expect to pay for a starter, main course, salad and house wine or water for one:
£ under 100kn   ££ 100kn–200kn   £££ over 200kn

LIMSKI KANAL

Fjord ££
The restaurant is above the jetty where boats from Poreč and Rovinj call before continuing their journey. There are lovely views over the bay from the large terrace. The menu includes fresh fish and seafood from the estaury as well as exceptionally good and cheap *čevapčići* which is served with chips, raw onions and *avjar*.
➕ 198 A4 ✉ Limski Kanal, nahe Kloštar
☎ 052 448 222 ⏰ Daily 11–10

MOTOVUN, BUZET AND GROŽNJAN

Humska Konoba £
This tiny, rustic inn is behind the town gate at the entrance to Hum that has a population of just 23. It serves typically Istrian dishes such as *fuži* with goulash and roast lamb, *supa*, an Istrian speciality of red wine warmed in a jug and served with sugar, pepper, olive oil and toast and its own *biska* (mistletoe brandy).
➕ 198 C4 ✉ Hum 2 ☎ 052 660 005
⏰ Jun–Oct daily 11–10, weekends only in winter

Konoba Mondo ££
This stylish restaurant, just outside the Old Town gates of Motovun, serves a number of truffle specialities, ranging from a simple black truffle omelette to more unusual dishes such as polenta and truffles, sheep's cheese or delicious fillet of beef with truffle sauce. It has a cosy, romantic atmosphere, with candlelit tables and whitewashed stone walls. On warm days you can eat on the terrace.
➕ 198 B4 ✉ Ulica Barbacan 1, Motovun
☎ 052 681 791
⏰ Mar–Nov Tue–Sun 12:30–3:30, 6:30–10

Stara Oštarija ££
The old village inn on the church square in Buzet reopened in 2005 as a classy restaurant, offering Istrian staples such as *maneštra* (vegetable soup), pasta, *ombolo* (pork fillet) and steak with truffles, as well as the local speciality *frittata* (truffle omelette), all accompanied by a selection of Istrian wines. For dessert, try *dolce Istriano*, a home-made cake. The restaurant is in a fabulous setting high above the cliffs and has wonderful views over the new town below.
➕ 198 B5 ✉ Ulica Petra Flega 5, Buzet
☎ 052 694 003 ⏰ Daily noon–10

Toklarija £££
From the outside, this looks like an old stone cottage, but it is in fact one of the most exclusive restaurants in Istria, located in a restored oil mill in a tiny hilltop hamlet above the Mirna valley. Don't bother coming to Toklarija if all you want is a quick, light snack This restaurant specialises in 'slow food' and most visitors have five courses, consisting of soup, cured ham, pasta, a main course and a dessert. Reservation is essential.
➕ 198 B4 ✉ Sovinjsko Polje 11 (off the main road from Buzet to Motovun)
☎ 052 663 031 ⏰ Wed–Mon 1pm–10pm

Zigante £££
People come from Zagreb, Italy and Slovenia in autumn to visit this

famous restaurant belonging to the Zigante Tartufi chain of truffle shops (➤ 114). It is in the village of Livade, near Motovun, among the oak forests of the Mirna valley, where Istria's truffles are found. Not surprisingly, truffles feature in almost every dish, with a choice of truffle-tasting menus at a range of prices. You can even have a refreshing truffle ice cream for pudding.

🔢 198 B4 ✉ Livade 7 ☎ 052 664 302
🕐 Daily noon–11

Le Mandrać £££

Situated at the end of the Lungomare promenade, with a terrace overlooking the fishing harbour at Volosoko, Le Mandrać takes the freshest local produce and gives it an unexpectedly creative twist. Seafood appears as sashimi or octopus gazpacho, while mussels come in a soup with Istrian ham and lemon leaf. If you want to splash out, go for the nine-course tasting menu that comprises small portions of seasonal specialities. Opened in 2004, Le Mandrać restaurant has won awards for its original approach to Croatian cuisine.

🔢 199 D4 ✉ Obala Frana Supila 10, Volosko
☎ 051 701 357; www.lemandrac.com
🕐 Daily noon–11

PULA

Konoba Batelina £££

It all started as a simple restaurant run by a fisherman's family. Konoba – 10km (6.3mi) from Pula – however has now advanced to become one of the most highly-acclaimed restaurants in Istria. The chef, David, only serves fish and seafood that his father, Danilo, catches that morning in the Adriatic. He defies the trend towards exotic fish through the creative way he serves creatures of the sea that, in other gourmet restaurants, would not necessarily even find their way into the kitchen. As a result, guests can indulge in sardines, pasta with dried fish roe or sharks' liver. The eloquent and incredibly friendly waiters are also happy to recommend Croatian sashimi or crab, depending on the season.

🔢 198 B2 ✉ Čimulje 25, Banjole
☎ 052 5 737 670 🕐 Mon–Sat 5pm–11pm

ROVINJ

La Puntulina £££

Perched at the tip of the Old Town above the popular bathing rocks, La Puntulina offers the most romantic setting in Rovinj, with a balcony overlooking the sea. By day, the terraces provide perfect platforms for sunbathing; at night, they turn into a fashionable wine bar where people gather to watch the sunset. The emphasis is on creative Istrian and Italian cuisine, such as carpaccio of sea bass or sole with truffles. There is also a four-course tasting menu on offer at La Puntulina with fresh seafood and pasta.

🔢 198 A3 ✉ Ulica Svetog Križa 38
☎ 052 813 186 🕐 Daily noon–3, 6–midnight

Veli Jože ££

This old-style konoba (tavern) on the waterfront is a cut above most of the tourist-oriented restaurants around the harbour. The interior is faux rustique, with wooden benches and walls covered in old farm tools, musical instruments and even a bicycle. In summer there are communal tables outside at the top of the harbour steps. The menu offers authentic Istrian cuisine – cured ham, sheep's cheese, grilled vegetables, pasta dishes, fuži (pasta) with goulash, roast lamb with potatoes and an excellent steak with truffles. This place is deservedly popular, so go early or be prepared to wait in order to get one of the outdoor tables.

🔢 198 A3 ✉ Ulica Svetog Križa 1
☎ 052 816 337 🕐 Mar–Dec daily 11am–1am

Where to ...
Shop

The local farmer Giancarlo Zigante earned himself a place in the *Guinness Book of World Records* when he found the world's biggest white truffle, weighing 1.31kg (2.9 lb), near Buje in 1999.

His fame spread throughout Istria and he is now the owner of a chain of shops, **Zigante Tartufi**, specialising in all things tuberiferous. In addition to fresh black and white truffles, the shops sell a wide range of truffle-based products, such as minced truffles, truffle oil, truffles with olives, truffles with mushrooms, *tartufata* (truffle paste) and sheep's cheese flavoured with truffles. The staff can offer advice, recipes and can gift wrap your own selection.

Zigante Tartufi shops also sell other Istrian food and drink products such as honey, wine and *biska* (mistletoe brandy). The main shop is in Buzet, beneath the entrance to the Old Town on Trg Fontana (open daily 9–8, tel: 052 663 340). There are other shops in Buje, Grožnjan, Livade, Motovun and Pula, or you can buy online under www.zigantetartufi.com

Next to the Grožnjan shop is a wine bar, located in an old Venetian loggia where you can sample local wines and truffle-based snacks. The Livade shop also has a restaurant attached (► 113).

Istrian wines, spirits and Zigante Tartufi products are available from **Eva** (Ulica Veli Jože 4, Motovun) and **Baccus** (Via Carrera 5, Rovinj).

Insider Tip

Rovinj is well known for its **artists** who proffer their works in the narrow streets of the Old Town.

Where to ...
Go Out

Summer evenings on the Istrian coast are so mild and pleasant that, for most people, the entertainment consists simply in being outdoors, joining the *korzo* (evening walk) around the squares and streets and enjoying the atmosphere in one of the many open-air cafés.

MUSIC

During the summer, look out for concerts in the churches and squares of Poreč, Rovinj and Pula.

In Poreč, classical concerts are held in the **Euphrasian Basilica**, in Rovinj, in the Church of St Euphemia and the **Franciscan monastery** and in Pula, in the magnificent setting of the Roman arena. Recitals also take place in summer in other coastal towns such as Umag, Novigrad and Vrsar and jazz concerts are held in the town museum courtyard in Poreč.

In inland Istria, the hill town of Grožnjan plays host each summer to **Jeunesses Musicales Croatia**, an international summer school of young musicians. You can ask at any tourist office for details of what's on locally, or keep an eye out for posters in the street.

FILM FESTIVALS

Pula and Motovun both host international film festivals in July, with a mixture of Croatian, foreign and avant-garde films.

Ask at tourist offices or see: http://pulafilmfestival.hr or www.motovunfilmfestival.com.

North and Central Dalmatia

 **Little Treats**

Dine like the locals

First of all you can sample the fresh fish at
Konoba Marija near **Murvica on Brač** (➤ 134)
before leaping into the crystal-clear sea.

Listening and watching

In the evening, the residents of **Zadar** (➤ 137)
are drawn to the Riva, where old and young
enjoy the 'sea organ' and the sunset.

The Robinson Crusoe experience

A boat trip around the **Kornati** archipelago
(➤ 138) highlights just what people had
to do without in days of old.

Getting Your Bearings

Dalmatia appears on the map as a long, thin coastal strip between the Adriatic and the Dinaric Alps. This is where you will find some of the most familiar images of Croatia – harbour towns dominated by Venetian-style *campanile*, lavender-scented islands fringed by impossibly blue seas. The northern islands around Zadar are some of the most unspoilt in the Adriatic while further south, around Split, islands such as Brač and especially Hvar are becoming increasingly fashionable with visitors.

Historically, Dalmatia has always been separate from Croatia and the region bears the hallmarks of its conquerors. The Greeks established trading colonies at Hvar (Pharos) and Vis (Issa), introducing vineyards still in use today. The Romans built a town at Salona, the emperor Diocletian was born here and later retired to Split where his palace forms the nucleus of the modern city. The Venetians ruled Dalmatia for almost 400 years, leaving behind beautiful churches and theatres at Šibenik, Trogir and Hvar. More recently, northern Dalmatia became a battleground in the war of 1991–95, when Serbian troops established the Republic of the Serbian Krajina at Knin, cutting off Dalmatia from the rest of Croatia. Today, the war-time damage has largely been repaired. Further inland, however, beyond Zadar and Šibenik, deserted houses are reminders of the clashes. The blossoming tourist industry quickly brought normality and wealth back to the coastal areas.

Touring Dalmatia is relatively easy. Most of the main sights are on the Magistrala coastal highway, while regular car and passenger ferries connect each of the islands to the mainland.

Map labels: Gospić, Ondić, Karlobag, Pag, Nacionalni Park Paklenica, Gračac, Silba, Olib, Pag, Vir, Premuda, Ist, Molat, 42 Nin, Posedarje, Kruševo, Škarda, Sestrunj, 43 Zadar, Ugljan, Benkovac, Iž, Dugi Otok, Pašman, 44 Vransko Jezero, Žut, Murter, Kornat, 45 Nacionalni Park Kornati

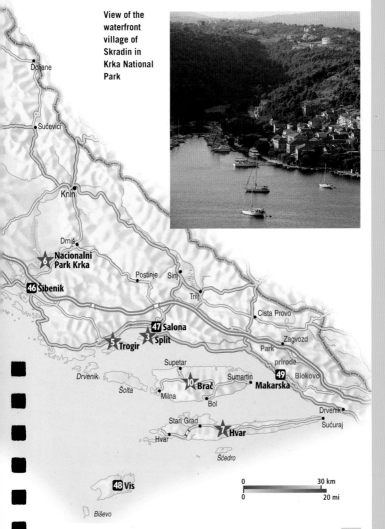

View of the waterfront village of Skradin in Krka National Park

117

Four Perfect Days

Perfect Days in...

If you're not quite sure where to begin your trip, this itinerary recommends a practical and enjoyable four-day tour of North and Central Dalmatia. For more information see the main entries (▶120).

Day 1

Morning
Make an early start to explore ⭐**Nacionalni Park Krka** (▶128), walking around the waterfalls and taking the boat trip up-river to the monastery at Visovac with lunch at Roški Slap.

Afternoon and evening
Drive down to 🔢**Šibenik** (below, ▶138) where St. Jacob's Catherdral is doubtlessly the major attraction. Then take the coast road to the medieval town of ⭐**Trogir** (▶125). Enjoy a sunset drink at one of the cafés on the Riva, then stroll around the Old Town before dinner.

Day 2

Morning
Don't leave Trogir without seeing the cathedral, with its magnificent carved Romanesque portal. Afterwards, you can make the short journey by car or local bus to ⭐**Split** (below ▶120).

Afternoon and evening
Take your time admiring the ruins of Diocletian's Palace, then stroll around the harbour and climb to the Marjan peninsula for woodland walks and sea views. Pause on the way down at Caffe Vidilica, whose terrace offers panoramic views over the city. Later, you can observe the evening *korzo* from a waterfront bar on the Riva. After dinner at Kod Jože (▶145), it is a short walk to the bus station for the ride back to Trogir.

Day 3

Morning

Return to Split and head down to the harbour to catch the ferry to Supetar on ⭐ **Brač** (▶ 134). From here, you can make a scenic tour of the island on your way to the south coast. Take the road through the pine woods to the summit of Vidova Gora for views over Brač and Hvar. If you are feeling hungry, there is a restaurant at the summit.

Afternoon and evening

Continue to Bol and walk along the promenade to Zlatni Rat for a lazy afternoon on the beach (above). A 4km (2.5-mile) clifftop path leads to Murvica where you will find Konoba Marija, one of Dalmatia's most spectacularly located restaurants (▶ 144)!

Day 4

Morning

In summer, take a taxi or excursion boat from Bol to Jelsa on ⭐ **Hvar** (▶ 130) where you can pick up a bus to Hvar Town. Otherwise the best way of travelling between islands is to return to Split and take the ferry to Hvar Town or Stari Grad. If you want to drive, you must go to Stari Grad; cars are not allowed to disembark at Hvar Town.

Afternoon and evening

Spend the rest of the day soaking up the atmosphere of Hvar Town, climbing to its citadel and relaxing on its beaches. A visit to the historical theatre Hvarsko Kazalište (▶ 146) is something very special.

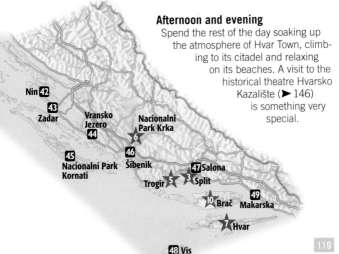

Nin **42**

43 Zadar

Vransko Jezero **44**

Nacionalni Park Krka **6**

45 Nacionalni Park Kornati

46 Šibenik

Trogir **5**

47 Salona

3 Split

10 Brač

49 Makarska

Hvar

48 Vis

⭐3 Split

Croatia's second city is built around the ruins of the Roman emperor Diocletian's palace (reigned 284–305AD). Cruise liners and ferries come and go in the harbour, the main point of departure for the Dalmatian islands.

Many visitors get their first view of Split as they sail into the harbour, with the palm trees and terrace cafés along the sea promenade against a backdrop of the tower blocks in the expanding modern city. This image perfectly captures the appeal of Split, a lively port city with an intriguing blend of ancient monuments and modern life. Nowhere is this more true than in the heart of the city, inside the walls of Diocletian's palace.

View of
Split from
the harbour

Diocletian's Palace

Diocletian was born c. 236–245AD in Salona. He was the son of slaves but rose to become emperor of Rome at the age of 39. He was notorious for his persecution of Christians; among those martyred under his rule were St Maurus, bishop of Poreč (➤ 97) and St Euphemia, patron saint of Rovinj (➤ 101). An innovative ruler, Diocletian divided up the empire and introduced the concept of retirement, returning to his native Dalmatia in 305 and living out his later years in this garrison town not far from Salona, present day Solin, surrounded by the walls and towers of a splendid imperial palace that he had commissioned. He died here around 312.

As early as the 7th century, people fleeing Salona took refuge in the palace and it has provided a home for local families ever since. These days little of the original remains and a lot of imagination is needed to make out the shape of the former Roman palace.

OTHER SIGHTS

■ Follow the seafront west for 30 minutes or take bus no. 7, 8 or 12 from the Riva to reach **Galerija Meštrović** (May–Sep Tue–Sun 9–7, Oct–Apr Tue–Sat 9–4, Sun 9–3, 30kn), a museum and sculpture garden in the former seaside villa of the sculptor Ivan Meštrović. The ticket is also valid for the **Holy Cross Chapel**, built by Meštrović to display his 'Life of Christ' cycle.

■ Climb the steps on Senjska at the west end of the Riva to reach the **Marjan peninsula**, a green hill with woodland walks, hermits' chapels and caves and views out to sea to the islands of Šolta, Brač, Hvar and Vis. For a two-hour round walk, follow the clifftop path for 2km (1.2mi) to the **chapel of St Hieronymus** and return via the summit at Telegrin (178m/584ft). On the way down, stop at Caffe Vidilica with views over the city and port from the terrace.

Insider Tip

Palace architecture

You enter from the Riva through the **Bronze Gate** which gives access to the **podrum** or underground chambers. This is the best surviving part of the original palace and it gives a good idea of the ground plan, as these rooms were directly beneath the imperial quarters above.

From the gallery you can climb the steps to the **peristyle**, the central courtyard of the palace and main square of the complex. The black granite sphinx, guarding the emperor's mausoleum, dates from 1500BC and was one of 12 sphinxes from ancient Egypt that once stood here; the rest were beheaded by Christians who saw them as symbols of the pagan emperor. The octagonal mausoleum was transformed in the 8th century into a **cathedral** (Jun–Sep daily 8–7, Oct–May 8–noon, 4–7), now an extraordinary blend of Roman, Romanesque and Gothic architecture. A frieze with relief work on the beams below the dome

Cafés and restaurants line the outer walls of Diocletian's Palace

An Imperial Retreat

Diocletian's Palace marks the beginnings of Split's history. Around 200AD Emperor Diocletian had a residence built for his retirement in the region he came from. The huge fortress-like palace has long since become an integral part of the Old Town. Nevertheless, large parts have survived that testify to the quality of Roman architecture.

The palace was abandoned at the end of the Ancient Roman era and was later used by the people of Salona (Solin) who had to flee from the Avars after their town was besieged. Above, in and around the Roman buildings a town was created which has remained virtually unaltered to this day.

❶Porta aenea: The palace complex is entered from the sea promenade through the Bronze Gate. Beyond it is a labyrinth of rooms which are no longer in their original form.

❷Podrum: These barrel vaulted rooms are now used for exhibitions.

❸Sveti Duje Cathedrale: This octagonal building from Antiquity, surrounded by a colonnade, was inaugurated in the 8th century as a Christian house of worship and raised to the status of a cathedral for the bishopric of Split in the mid 10th century.

❹Sveti Rok: St Rok's Church (now the Tourist Information Office and souvenir shop), on the eastern side of the peristyle, dates from the 16th century and has a lovely Renaissance façade.

❺Sveti Filip: The church of St Philip Neri on Kraljice Square was built in 1735 by the Venetian architect Franceso Melchiori.

❻Peristyle: This elongated square is bordered on both its longer sides by arches supported on columns with Corinthian capitals. Behind the columns on the southern (shorter) side are the emperor's private chambers. During the Renaissance and Baroque eras two chapels were added.

❼Papalić Palace: The town residence of the Papalić family now houses the Municipal Museum. The Roman palace was rebuilt in the 15th century by Juraj Dalmatinac in the Venetian Gothic style.

❽Agubio and Cindro Palace: Features of Gothic and Renaissance architecture can be seen in these patricians' palaces in Krešimirova and Dioklecijanova ulica.

❾Porta aurea: In the early Middle Ages St Martin's Chapel was added in the Old Croatian style in the outer walkway over the Golden Gate at the northern entrance to the town.

❿Porta ferrea: The Iron Gate provides access to the Old Town from the west. The bell tower dates from the 11th century.

⓫Ninski Monument: The stutue of Bishop Grgur Ninski (Gregor of Nin) right in front of the Porta aurea was made by Ivan Meštrović.

The peristyle served a representative function at the emperor's day; now it is a popular place where people congregate, especially in summer

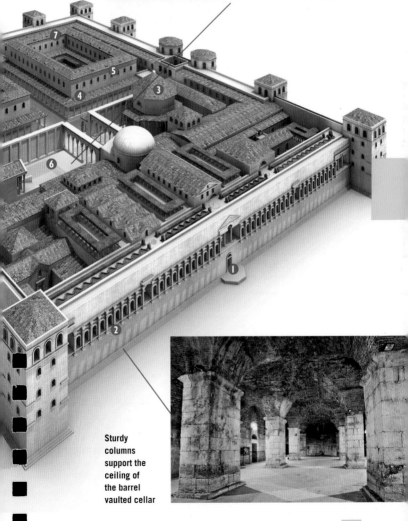

Sturdy columns support the ceiling of the barrel vaulted cellar

depicts Eros out hunting, together with portraits of Diocletian and his wife Prisca. There are altars to the saints Domnius and Anastasius, both martyred by Diocletian and now commemorated in his cemetery. You can climb the adjoining bell tower for views over the port and the palace complex.

Insider Tip

A lane opposite the cathedral leads to the Roman **Temple of Jupiter**, now the **baptistry**, whose 11th-century font is adorned with a relief of King Zvonimir, said to be the first European king immortalised in stone. Follow the Cardo, the main north–south axis of the palace and leave through the Golden Gate, beyond which you will find a huge bronze sculpture by Ivan Meštrović (➤ 54). It depicts Grgur Ninski (Gregory of Nin), a 9th-century bishop who campaigned for the use of the Slavic language and Glagolitic script to replace Latin in churches. There are copies of the statue in Varaždin and in Nin itself, but this is the original.

Twelve sphinxes once guarded the emperor's mausoleum

TAKING A BREAK

The **waterfront cafés** on the Riva make a good place to relax at any time of day.

✚ 203 E3

Tourist Information Office
✉ Crkvica Svetog Roka, Peristil ☎ 021 345 606; www.visitsplit.com

Podrum
🕐 Summer Mon–Sat 9–9, Sun 9–6, winter Mon–Sat 9–2 💳 25kn

Jupiter Temple
🕐 Mon–Sat 7–noon, 5–7 💳 10kn

INSIDER INFO

The biggest **market**, selling fresh fruit, vegetables, bread and cheese, can be found outside the eastern Silver Gate in Diocletian's Palace.

In more depth The **Archaeological Museum** (Jun–Sep Mon–Sat 9–2, 4–8, Oct–May Mon–Fri 9–2, 4–8, Sat 9–2, 20kn), a short walk north of central Split, is the oldest museum in Croatia. It features Greek and Roman objects, including wine jars and oil lamps from Vis and marble figures of Roman gods, jewellery and ceramics as well as gifts placed in graves from the Roman city of Salona (➤ 139).

⭐Trogir

Founded by Greek settlers in the 3rd century BC on an oval-shaped island, separated from the mainland by a narrow channel, the town is now a relaxing place of cafés, yachts and car-free streets, with a beautiful cathedral at its heart.

The Old Town is connected to the mainland by a bridge, giving easy access to the 17th-century **Kopnena Vrata** (Land Gate), an archway topped by a statue of St John of Trogir, a 12th-century bishop by the name of Giovanni Orsini who is considered the patron saint and protector of the town.

The Old Town

From here you enter a maze of narrow streets and cobbled lanes, full of trendy shops, restaurants and art galleries. This is a town for strolling around, looking for architectural details as you come across courtyards, churches and palaces. The one unmissable sight is the **cathedral**, begun in the 13th century and adorned with a Venetian Gothic *campanile* that was added in various stages up to the 16th century. The west portal, carved in 1240 by Master Radovan, is perhaps the finest piece of Romanesque art in Croatia – a riot of saints and angels mixed with scenes from everyday life and the seasons of the year, illustrated through rural activities such as the grape harvest and the

Exquisite ornamentation, rich in detail, decorates the west portal of Trogir Cathedral

The Town Hall clock tower in Trogir

annual pig slaughter. The upper archway depicts the Nativity, while the pillars to either side feature Adam and Eve standing on a pair of lions. There are more treasures inside the cathedral, including a 13th-century octagonal stone pulpit, carved wooden choirstalls and the 15th-century chapel of St John of Trogir, with its sculpted angels and cherubs, scallop-shell niches and an elaborately carved sarcophagus.

Next to the cathedral, the town hall displays a plaque recording Trogir's designation as a UNESCO World Heritage Site in 1997. On the other side of the square is a Venetian loggia, once used as the town court, with a 15th-century relief of Justice by Nikola Firentinac, the architect of St John's Chapel.

Gradska, the main street, leads down to the **Gradska Vrata** (Town Gate) and gives access to the Riva, a pleasant promenade with views across the water to the island of Čiovo. From here you can make a complete circuit of the island, passing 15th-century Kamerlengo fortress.

TAKING A BREAK

There are numerous cafés and ice-cream parlours on the **Riva** and in the streets and squares around the cathedral.

🕂 203 E3

left: Boats moored in the harbour in Trogir

Tourist Information Office
✉ Ivana Pavla II ☎ 021 885 628, http://tztrogir.hr

Cathedral
🕑 Summer Mon–Sat 8–6, Sun 2–6, winter Mon–Sat 8–noon 🎟 24kn

INSIDER INFO

- Arriving by car, drive over the bridge to **Čiovo** and park on the far side, then walk back to Trogir, with fine views of the Old Town on its island as you approach.
- Climb the tower of **Kamerlengo fortress** (summer daily 9–7, 10kn) for the best views over the town.
- Trogir makes a good base for visiting **Split** (▶ 120); buses depart several times a day from the bus stop next to the bridge in the Old Town.
- In summer, ferries operated by **Jadrolinija** (▶ 38) leave from the Riva for the solitary islands and bays of Veli Drvenik and Mali Drvenik
- An unsual eye-catcher can be seen above portal of the Dominican church on the Riva – a **carved relief of the Virgin Mary**, accompanied by Mary Magdalene, naked apart from her hair flowing down to her feet.

★ Nacionalni Park Krka

If you make only one trip away from the Dalmatian coast, it should be to Krka National Park. Here, you can swim beneath cascading waterfalls and take a boat trip through a limestone canyon to visit a remote island monastery.

The Krka River runs for 72km (45mi) from its source in the foothills of the Dinaric mountains near Knin to its mouth at Šibenik. For much of its length, it flows through narrow gorges, forming waterfalls and lakes rivalling those at Plitvice (► 72) for their beauty.

You can visit the park by bus from **Šibenik**, or on an organised excursion from one of the coastal resorts. The classic approach is from the waterfront village of Skradin, where national park boats (included in the entry fee) ferry you into the park along a wooded gorge. The boats arrive near a wooden footbridge beneath the falls at **Skradinski Buk**, the most dramatic sight in the park, which drop 45m (147ft) in a series of 17 steps. In summer, you are allowed to swim in the shallow pool at the base of the falls. From here, an easy two-hour circuit leads on foot around the cascades.

The alternative entrance is via **Lozovac** where there is a large car park and shuttle buses ferrying visitors to the top

The secluded island monastery on Lake Viscovac

Take a refreshing dip at the Skradinski Buk waterfalls

of the falls. This is a spectacular journey, with superb views over the river. It is still possible to do the two-hour circuit of the falls on foot. From November to February, when the boats and buses do not operate, you can drive to the top of the falls from Lozovac or take your car to the foot of the falls from Skradin.

Boat trips

A kiosk near the shuttle bus stop sells tickets in summer for additional boat trips along the **Krka canyon**. The shortest journey (there and back: 2 hours) is to **Visovac**, a Franciscan monastery founded on a rocky islet in the river in 1445. The museum contains an illustrated 15th-century Croatian version of *Aesop's Fables*, one of only three such books in the world (the others are in Oxford and Venice). Some of the boat trips (4 hours) continue to **Roški Slap**, a second set of waterfalls with a height of 22m (72ft).

Insider Tip

TAKING A BREAK

There are cafés at Roški Slap and Skradinski Buk, both at the top and bottom of the falls. **Kristijan**, in an old stone mill above the jetty at Roški Slap, serves excellent cured ham, cheese and olives and also sells home-made wine and brandy.

✚ 202 C4 ✉ 12km (7.5mi) north of Šibenik ☎ 022 201 777; www.npkrka.hr
🕐 Summer daily 8–8, winter 9–4 💶 Summer 110kn, winter 30kn

INSIDER INFO

- You can take a second boat trip upstream from Roški Slap to **Krka Orthodox monastery**, cruising through a dramatic canyon in the less visited northern reaches of the park. It may be possible to combine this with an excursion to **Roški Slap** (allow 6 hours in total), but it will probably mean spending a second day in the park and then driving to Roški Slap to begin your journey.

- Take your swimming things with you! In summer, the 🏊 **places where you can swim** at the Skradinski Buk waterfalls are invitingly refreshing!

Insider Tip

 Hvar

Hvar is among the most appealing of the Adriatic islands, blessed with a mild climate and covered with vineyards and lavender fields. Its capital of the same name has become the most fashionable spot on the entire Dalmatian coast.

The island of Hvar is a long, thin strip with a limestone ridge running along its centre and steep cliffs tumbling down towards isolated beaches and coves. In spring and early summer, the island is a blaze of colour and the soothing scent of lavender hangs in the air and is carried on the sea breeze. Even by Croatian standards, Hvar has a pleasing climate, with more hours of sunshine than anywhere else in the Adriatic.

The closest access from the mainland is the car ferry from Drvenik to Sucuraj, though this is followed by a long drive across the island to reach Hvar Town. Alternatively, you can take the ferry from Split to Stari Grad, the old capital.

Insider Tip Other options for foot passengers are a ferry from Split directly to Hvar Town, or a fast catamaran from Split to Jelsa in summer.

The cathedral looks over the main square in Hvar Town

Hvar Town

The best way to arrive in Hvar Town is by sea, from where it appears like a jumble of brown stone houses crowded around the shores of the bay, overlooked by its old castle and medieval walls. During the summer, the port is a hive of activity, with sleek yachts moored in the harbour, ferries disembarking passengers and taxi-boats taking sunbathers to the offshore islands. Although it has its monuments, this is really a town for relaxing more than anything else and the evening *korzo* is one of the liveliest in Croatia.

Café life focuses on **Trg Svetog Stjepana**, a Venetian-style piazza which opens out to the sea, with flagstoned paving and a 16th-century well. The west end is dominated by the cathedral and its four-storey *campanile*; notice how the number of arched windows increases on each level. At the seaward end of the square, next to the inner harbour, is the **Venetian arsenal**, built to allow entire galleys to enter for repairs. The top floor houses one of Europe's oldest public theatres that opened in 1612. Renovation work on the theatre has been going on for years and it can only be visited in the peak season (July, Aug 9–1, 3–11, 20kn).

Across the square, beyond the Renaissance palaces built by nobles in the 16th century, steps lead up to

the **Citadel** (in summer open daily 8am–midnight, 25kn), a Venetian fortress built in 1557. There is a small museum of *amphorae* and you can also clamber down and have a look at the prison cells. The real attraction however, is the stunning view out over the rooftops and out to the Pakleni Islands and Vis on the horizon.

🏛 Hvar Town beaches

A short walk south of the ferry dock leads to a Franciscan monastery, on a headland overlooking a small pebble cove. On the far side of the harbour, the seafront promenade continues westwards for some 2km (1.2mi), passing numerous rocky beaches and bathing platforms, popular with locals in summer.

For a lazy afternoon on the beach, a better option is to take a water-taxi to the **Pakleni Islands**, an emerald-green chain of islets just offshore from Hvar Town, with pine woods and remote pebble beaches. The nearest island, **Jerolim**, is used by nudists. On **Stipanska** you can relax during the day on fashionable Carpe Diem Beach and dance the night away to music played by hip DJs.

Insider Tip

Stari Grad

Until the Venetians moved the capital to Hvar Town in
the 13th century, Stari Grad was the largest settlement
on Hvar, founded by Greek settlers from Paros in the
4th century BC and named Pharos (from which Hvar is
derived). Its current name, Stari Grad, simply means
'Old Town'. Although not as chic as Hvar Town, it is
nevertheless attractive, in a sheltered bay beside the
island's chief ferry port.

The narrow cobbled streets behind the harbour are
great for strolling, exploring hidden gems like the 12th-
century **Chapel of St John**, with its 6th-century mosaics
set into the floor. Near here is the archaeological site
of Greek Pharos, where excavations are still going on.

Just back from the seafront, **Tvrdalj Petra Hektorovića**
(open summer daily 10–1, 5–7, 15kn) was the summer
home of the poet Petar Hektorović (1487–1572), designed
as a fortress where the townspeople could take refuge in
the event of a Turkish invasion. The walled garden, with its
fishpond and pomegranate trees, makes a good place to
sit and contemplate the Latin inscriptions with which the
poet adorned his home – such as the skull and crossbones
with the reminder 'Neither riches nor fame, beauty nor age
can save you from death'.

Jelsa

Hvar's third town, Jelsa, is on the north coast, looking
across towards Brač and the Makarska Rivijera. In summer,
this is undeniably a holiday town, with cafés on the promenade and rocky beaches with pine woods and hotels beyond.

Boats bob up
and down in
crystal-clear
water in the
harbour in
Hvar's Old
Town

INSIDER INFO

Stari Grad Plain (polje) – to the east of the town – has been a UNESCO World Heritage Site since 2008. The area that is still used for farming, is a cultivated landscape that has remained unspoilt since colonialisation by the Greeks in the 4th century BC.

In more depth The pebble beaches and coves of the south coast are much less developed than those in Hvar Town, Jelsa and Stari Grad. Get there by taking the road tunnel through the island's highest mountain, Sveti Nikola. The 8km (5mi) stretch between Sveta Nedjelja and Zavala passes isolated beaches and stone villages nestling beneath steep hillsides planted with south-facing vineyards where much of Hvar's best wine is produced.

The most important site worth seeing is the 16th-century octagonal **Chapel of St John**, in a narrow lane behind the port. A 4km (2.5-mile) coastal path leads to the fishing village of Vrboska, a laid-back resort with some good beaches on the Glavica peninsula. Water-taxis make the trip from Jelsa to **Vrboska** in summer and to the islet of **Zečevo**, with its nudist beaches. If you feel like a change of scene, there are also excursion boats in the harbour offering day-trips to the famous Zlatni Rat beach on Brač (► 135).

Colourful fields of lavender on Hvar

Insider Tip

TAKING A BREAK

The harbourside in Hvar Town seems to be one endless promenade in summer and most visitors spend hours just sitting at waterfront cafés and bars watching life go by and looking out for celebrities on their yachts. **Ulica Petra Hektorovića**, one flight up towards the castle on the north side of the main square, is Hvar's trendy restaurant quarter, with a choice of three classy establishments on the same street (► 144).

➕ 204 A3

Tourist Information Office
✉ Trg Svetog Stjepana
☎ 021 742 977; www.tzhvar.hr

 Brač

**The largest island off the Dalmatian coast, Brač is a place of super-
latives – from the highest mountain in the Adriatic you look down
on Croatia's most famous beach – and it is easily reached by ferry
in under an hour from Split.**

The most popular way of getting to Brač is on the regular
car ferry from Split to Supetar. In summer, there are
fast catamarans which make the journey direct from Split
to Bol on the south coast. Ferries also run throughout
the year from Makarska on the mainland to Sumartin on
the eastern tip of the island. In addition, Brač is the
only Dalmatian island with its own airport, with connecting
flights to Zagreb in summer.

Its easy accessibility means that Brač attracts the crowds,
but out of season it is a peaceful island of vineyards,
orchards and fishing villages hiding in sheltered bays.
The island is famous for its white limestone which has
been quarried here since Roman times and used in buildings as diverse as Diocletian's palace in Split and the
White House in Washington DC. Even today, you will notice
that many of the houses on Brač, built of local stone, seem
to have an extra sheen.

Zlanti Rat
is one of the
best-known
and most
beautiful
beaches
in Croatia

Arriving in Brač

Most visitors will arrive in **Supetar**, the largest town on the
island, but little more than a village with low-rise houses
around the harbour. There is plenty of activity by the port

when the ferries come in, but at other times this is a sleepy place where many people from Split have their summer homes. Most of the hotels are to the west of town, where several pebble beaches face across the water towards Split.

The main road crosses the island from north to south, with a side road leading up through the pine woods to the summit of **Vidova Gora** (778m/2552ft), the highest mountain on any of the Adriatic islands. The peak is marked by a white stone cross; from here there are fabulous views over Zlatni Rat beach to the islands of Hvar and Korčula. It is also possible to hike up here from Bol on a well-marked path.

Bol

Bol nestles beneath the southern slopes of Vidova Gora and is the only town on the south coast. Throughout summer, this is where the action is, with day-trippers from Hvar flocking to its beaches and tour operators advertising boat trips, windsurfing, sailing, scuba diving and free climbing (rock climbing without ropes and equipment).

The attraction here is 🎯 **Zlatni Rat** (Golden Cape or Horn), easily the most photographed beach in Croatia, on a triangular spit of fine shingle which juts 300m (985ft) out to sea, with shady pine woods at its centre. You can get there by walking along the 2km (1.2-mile) promenade that leads to the west from the harbour at Bol. Zlatni Rat is deservedly popular and it does get extremely busy in summer; to escape the crowds, you'll have to head for the rocky coves beyond, some of which are popular among nudists. *Insider Tip*

Dragon's Cave

Beyond Zlatni Rat, an unmade road leads along the cliff top, arriving after 4km (2.5mi) in the village of **Murvica** where you will find the restaurant Konoba Marija (► 144). In the hills above Murvica is the extraordinary **Zmajeva Špilja** (Dragon's Cave) where dragons and mythical creatures have been carved into the rock, probably by 16th-century monks who sheltered here before founding the hermitage at **Blaca**. To visit the cave, call the guide (tel: 091 5 149 787) and he will arrange to meet you at the restaurant if he is free. Guided tours of the cave are also organised by the Tourist Information Office in

Costal view from Bol to Murvica

Insider Tip

Bol. It is possible to get there on your own, but you will have to make do with staring at the carvings from outside the gate. Climb the path to the top of the village and follow the red arrows east for about an hour. It's a gentle ascent at first, but is followed by a steep climb up the hill to a ruined 18th-century monastery. From here, the Dragon's Cave is now about 200m to your left.

TAKING A BREAK

There are plenty of cafés next to the harbour in **Bol** and on the beach at **Zlatni Rat** in summer. For lunch with a particularly good view, try **Konoba Marija** (► 144) or **Vidova Gora** (summer daily 10am–midnight, tel: 021 549 061), on the summit of Vidova Gora.

✚ 203 F2

Tourist Information Office
☎ 021 635 638; www.bol.hr

INSIDER INFO

- The island's only sandy beach is at 🔟 **Lovrečina**, 5km (3mi) from the village of Postira on the north coast.
- The 16th-century **hermitage at Blaca** can be reached along a 12km (7.5-mile) coastal path from Zlatni Rat or a rough track leading off the road to Vidova Gora. In summer, local tour operators offer boat trips from Bol harbour to Blaca Bay, followed by a short uphill hike to the monastery (May–Oct Tue–Sun 9–5, 30kn).
- For a **scenic tour of northwest Brač**, take the coast road from Supetar to Sutivan, then head inland to the pretty village of Ložišća, high above a gorge. The main road continues down to the sea at Milna, set in a sheltered bay where yachts are often moored in summer. To return to Supetar, turn left in Ložišća and follow the narrow ridge to Nerežišća, passing marble quarries on the way.

At Your Leisure

42 Nin

Crossing the stone bridge and walking through the entrance gate of this single-street town, built on an island in the lagoon at Dalmatia's northern tip, you would never guess that this was once the ecclesiastical and royal capital of Croatia. Between the 9th and 12th centuries, seven kings were crowned here and the bishop of Nin was the most powerful religious figure in the land. One famous bishop, Gregory of Nin, was immortalised in bronze by Ivan Meštrović; the original sculpture is in Split (➤ 124) but a copy is on display in Nin.

The greatest treasure of Nin is the 9th-century **Church of the Holy Cross**, a simple, whitewashed, domed chapel in the form of a Greek cross which is sometimes claimed to be the world's smallest cathedral. It stands all alone on a grassy spot in the middle of town, surrounded by the ruins of a **Roman temple**.

Almost as spectacular is the **Church of St Nicholas**, built on a small burial mound 1km (half a mile) out of Nin on the road to **Zadar**. Also dating from the 9th century, it is topped by a **16th-century tower** added by the Venetians during their battles with the Turks. **Sabunike**, 2km (1.2mi) north of Nin, has one of the finest sandy beaches in Croatia, with views to **Pag** and the **Velebit massif** across the water.

Insider Tip

➕ 202 C3

Tourist Information Office
✉ Trg Braće Radića 3 ☎ 023 265 247, www.nin.hr

43 Zadar

The second-largest town in Dalmatia came under the rule of the Croatian-Hungarian monarchy from the mid 11th century onwards. Later, it put up a bold resistance against power-hungry Venice even though this was in vain. These days, it is a strange mixture of sprawling suburbs and picturesque Old Town squeezed onto a narrow peninsula still partly enclosed by its medieval walls. Largely destroyed by Allied bombs during World War II, the Old Town has been heavily modernised, with the result that brutal concrete architecture and shopping arcades are found side by side with **ancient churches** and cobbled streets.

At the heart of it all is the old **Roman Forum**. Stone from here was used to build **St Donat's Church**, a lovely 9th-century Byzantine round church dedicated to an Irish bishop of Zadar who is said to have built it himself (summer daily 9–8). Next to the church is the 12th-century **Romanesque cathedral**; you can climb the bell tower for stunning views. Also on the Forum is the church and convent of St Mary. The treasury contains an **exhibition of religious art** with extravagantly ornamental reliquaries produced by the town's gold and silversmiths and a reconstruction of an 11th-century chapel (summer Mon–Sat 10–1, 6–8, Sun 10–noon, winter Mon–Sat 10–1, 20kn).

Zadar's most recent attractions are to be found along the Riva, the sea promenade. **Morske Orgulje** is a 'sea organ' made up of steps going down to the water's edge. Behind these, out of sight, are a number of pipes from which sounds, caused by the waves, are emitted. Next to this is a circular, solar-battery operated installation called 'Greeting to the Sun' (Pozdrav suncu) that is set into the ground and shines at night. Both works of

North and Central Dalmatia

art were made by an architect from Zadar, Nicola Bašić, and have become a popular place to head for during the evening *korzo*.

Ferries leave from Zadar for the peaceful, unspoiled islands of **Ugljan**, **Pašman** and **Dugi Otok** (Long Island).

➕ 202 C2

Tourist Information Office
✉ Narodni Trg 5 ☎ 023 316 166, www.tzzadar.hr

44 Vransko Jezero

Croatia's largest natural lake is 25km (15.5mi) south of Zadar, just inland from the beach resorts of **Biograd** and **Pakoštane**. Since 1999, the entire lake has been designated a nature park, attracting more than 100 species of waterfowl in winter and a colony of purple herons to the **ornithological reserve** on its northwest shore. In summer, you can rent rowing boats to go out on the lake, or follow the 30km (18-mile) cycle trail around its shore.

➕ 202 B5

45 Nacionalni Park Kornati

A cruise through the Kornati Islands is unforgettable. Off the coast between Zadar and Šibenik, this is an ethereal seascape of cliffs, coves, underwater caves and rocky islets, described by the Irish playwright George Bernard Shaw (1856–1950) as having been created by the gods out of the stars and their own tears.

Kornati, a paradise for sailing enthusiasts

The Kornati National Park contains 89 islands and reefs, but the archipelago has over 140, stretching north as far as the spectacular **Telašcića Bay** on Dugi Otok. For most of the year, the islands are uninhabited, but in summer the residents of **Murter** set up fish restaurants in the bays and rent out stone cottages and fishing boats for a 'Robinson Crusoe' experience. The islands are a paradise for sailors and the best way to see them is on your own yacht, though tour operators also offer day excursions from **Murter**, **Zadar** and **Šibenik**.

Insider Tip

➕ 202 C1

Tourist Information Office
✉ Ulica Butina 2, Murter
☎ 022 435 740; www.kornati.hr
🕐 depending on the size of boat

46 Šibenik

Šibenik is without doubt one of the most beautiful towns in the whole of the eastern Adriatic. Its location alone, in a fjord-like bay, is especially lovely. The Old Town, that is well worth a visit, is dominated by the Cathedral of **St James** (➤ 140), that dates from the 15th-century. It stands proudly above the mouth of the **River Krka** and is perhaps the finest example of ecclesiastic architecture in Croatia. It is mostly the work of Juraj Dalmatinac (George the Dalmatian), a Zadar-born architect who trained in Venice; a sculpture of him by Ivan Meštrović stands on the cathedral square. After Dalmatinac's death

in 1473, the work was completed by Niccolò Fiorentino (Nicholas of Florence), who added the dome and the distinctive **barrel-vaulted roof**. The result is a harmonious blend of Venetian Gothic and Renaissance styles. The outer portals, sculpted by Dalmatinac, are full of florid detail.

Near here is Dalmatinac's playful masterpiece, the frieze of **74 stone heads** running around the exterior of the apse, depicting a fascinating cross-section of 15th-century society. They are said to be portraits of those citizens who refused to pay towards the cost of the cathedral. Inside the building, don't miss the tiny hidden **baptistry**, reached down a flight of steps to the right of the altar, with delicately carved stone angels beneath a vaulted roof.
🚩 202 C4 ✉ Trg Republike Hrvatske, Šibenik 🕙 Apr–Sep 8.30–8, winter 8.30–noon, 4–6:30 🎫 15kn

47 Salona
The most significant archaeological site in Croatia is also a highly atmospheric place, the **ruins of a Roman city** of 60,000 people surrounded by fields with the tower blocks of Split visible just below. In Roman times, this was the largest town on the coast, flourishing from the 2nd century BC up until the 5th century AD; the emperor Diocletian is thought to have been born here.

Just inside the entrance gate, the **necropolis of Manastirine** has the feel of an archaeological junk shop, with tombs and sarcophagi scattered among piles of stones. In the presbytery of a Roman basilica is the **vaulted tomb** of Domnius, the first bishop of Salona, executed in the nearby amphitheatre in 304AD during Diocletian's persecution of Christians.

From the **Tusculum archaeological museum**, a path leads to the lower town, based around the ruins of an impressive church. You can walk

Roman amphitheatre at Salona

along the Roman walls and into the fields to reach the well-preserved **amphitheatre**, with seating for 15,000 spectators. Many of the treasures from Salona are now on display in the Archaeological Museum at Split (➤ 125).
🚩 203 E3 ✉ 5km (3mi) from Split ☎ 021 212 900 🚌 Bus from Split 🕙 Summer Mon–Fri 7–7, Sat 9–7, Sun 9–1, winter Mon–Fri 9–3, Sat 9–2 🎫 10kn

48 Vis
One of Croatia's remotest inhabited islands was closed to foreigners from World War II until 1989, when it was used by the Yugoslav army as a military base. Apart from a few fishermen and winemakers, most of the islanders left during that time, but Vis is now reaping the benefit as, spared the impact of mass tourism, it is fast developing a reputation as a fashionable resort. Expensive yachts are moored in the harbour in summer and the island can now be reached daily by catamaran from Split in under two hours.

Insider Tip

It was the Greeks who founded the **settlement of Issa**, on the site of the present-day town of Vis in the 4th century BC; the remains of an **ancient Greek cemetery** lie just back from the harbour. Finds from Issa are exhibited in the museum that is housed in a former fort from

The Cathedral of St James, Šibenik

The Katedrala sv. Jakova was begun in 1431 and consecrated in 1556. The plain building boasts outstandingly beautiful stone carvings and has well-balanced and harmonious proportions. The construction of the dome and the barrel vaulting is unique. The marble slabs support their own weight and the builders did without mortar – the stone blocks being mortised to one another.

Limestone and marble from the island of Brač are the main building materials. To start with, the cathedral was the work of predominantly Italian architects. From the 1440s onwards, however, the local Master Builder and sculptor Juraj Dalmatinac took over the management of the stonemasons' workshop. The cross-shaped ground plan, the choir, the baptistry and the sacristy as well as the concept behind the crossing dome are his work.

❶ **Side portal:** The Master Builder took the portal flanked by lions from the first cathedral on this site and placed it on the east-facing side wall.

❷ **Roof:** Dalmatinac's pupil and successor, Niccolò Fiorentino, completed the building. The barrel-vaulted roof is made of stone slabs that interlock without the use of any bonding material.

❸ **Bishop Juraj Šižgorić's tomb:** Just to the right of the entrance, in the first bay, is the interesting tomb of the bishop and humanist Juraj Šižgorić. It was made in 1454 to a design by Dalmatinac.

❹ **Altar of the Three Kings:** The marble reliefs on this altar, in the second bay to the left of the entrance, are by Niccolò Fiorentino; the painting is the work of Bernardo Rizzardi.

❺ **Altar of the Holy Cross:** Located on the right before the crossing (between the nave and the choir), this altar was created by an artist from Split around the middle of the 15th century.

❻ **High altar:** The high altar and wooden pulpit are Baroque.

❼ **Baptistry:** A flight of narrow steps to the right of the crossing leads to the baptistry with four arched apses and a font. Andrija Aleši completed the work begun by Dalmatinac.

❽ **Treasury:** Works by the Šibenik goldsmith Horacije Fortezza from the 16th century are on display here.

74 sculpted portraits of Dalmation citizens, contemporaries of their creator Dalmatinac, line the apses in the choir

The stonemasons created a memorial to their own skill in the form of this magnificent rose window

North and Central Dalmatia

the Austro-Hungarian period. During the Napoleonic wars (1811–15), the island was occupied by the British who also had a base here during World War II when Tito briefly set up his headquarters in a cave on **Mount Hum**. Walk onto the cliffs on the west of the harbour to reach the abandoned George III fortress, from which thre are wonderful views over the bay towards Hvar in good weather.

On the far side of the bay, a stroll through the suburb of **Kut** leads to a small English cemetery, with memorials to victims of the Napoleonic wars and the 'comrades of Tito's liberation war'. Buses from the town of Vis make the journey across the island, passing vineyards and steep terraces on the way to the attractive fishing port of **Komiža**. This picturesque little place has kept its relaxed atmosphere unlike the busy main town on the island. There are many old buildings to be admired on a stroll through the narrow streets. The fishing museum in the fort illustrates the traditional methods used by local fishermen.

Insider Tip
In summer, boat trips are available from Komiža to the **Blue Grotto** (Modra Špilja) and the island of Biševo nearby. When the sun shines through a crack in the cliffs, lighting up the cave, the sea water in it turns a surreal, turquoise colour. Vis has a coastline with lots of bays. Dream beaches can often be reached on foot from both of the main roads across the island – such as Uvala Travna and Uvala Štinina that are both near Plisko Polje.
✚ 203 D1

Tourist Information Office
✉ Šetalište Stare Isse 5 ☎ 021 717 017, www.tz-vis.hr

⁴⁹⁵¹ Makarska

The string of beautiful, gently sloping pebbly beaches in the shadow of the **Biokovo Massif** is known as the **Makarska Rivijera**. Former fishing villages such as Brela, Baška Voda, Tučepi and Podgora are now attractive summer resorts, while the town of **Makarska**, set in a horse-shoe bay, gets very lively in high season. This is where package tourism has made the greatest impact in Dalmatia and Makarska certainly lacks the character and charm of some of the Venetian towns on this coast, although it does make a good base for a family holiday.

Looming over the coast is the table mountain of **Biokovo**, the summit of which – **Sveti Jure** (1,762m/5,781ft) – is the second highest in Croatia. Climb to Sveti Jure from Makarska for views stretching all the way to Italy on a clear day.
✚ 204 A4

Tourist Information Office
✉ Obala Kralja Tomislava 16 ☎ 021 612 002; www.makarska-info.hr

The Biokovo Massif lines the wonderful beaches of the Makarska Rivijera

Where to ...
Stay

Prices
Expect to pay per person per night for a double room in summer:
£ under 300kn   **££** 300kn–600kn   **£££** over 600kn

BRAČ

Palaca Dešković £££
This 15th-century palace next to the harbour at Pučišća has been converted by Countess Dešković into a small luxury hotel. The town is famous for its local marble.
✚ 203 F2 ✉ Pučišća
☎ 021 778 240; www.palaca-deskovic.com

HVAR

Riva/Palace £££
The Riva on the harbourside is a chic boutique hotel. It is also the first hotel in Croatia to become a member of the Small Luxury Hotels of the World group. It is under the same ownership as the Hotel Palace which is in the former Venetian governor's palace on the main square complete with clock tower and loggia. The Palace has tastefully furnished rooms with a neutral décor.
✚ 203 E2 ✉ Riva, Hvar Town
☎ 021 750 555; www.suncanihvar.com

NACIONALNI PARK KRKA

Skradinski Buk ££
Most people visit the waterfalls as a day trip from the coast, but to explore the national park in depth, stay at this family-run hotel, in a restored townhouse in the waterfront village of Skradin. The 28 rooms are simply furnished and painted in warm pastel shades and the third-floor terrace has river

Insider Tip

views. The jetty for shuttle boats to the national park is just 300m away.
✚ 202 C4 ✉ Burinovac, Skradin
☎ 022 771 771; www.skradinskibuk.hr

SPLIT

Peristil £££
The Peristil was the first hotel within the walls of Diocletian's Palace when it opened in 2005. The hotel is a curious blend of old and new, with modern facilities side by side with Roman arches and ancient stone walls.
✚ 203 E3 ✉ Poljana Kraljice Jelene 5
☎ 021 329 070; www.hotelperistil.com

TROGIR

Concordia ££
This 18th-century townhouse near Kamerlengo fortress is now a small hotel, with views across to the island of Čiovo. All 14 rooms have a shower, TV, air-conditioning. The hotel has its own car park.
✚ 203 E3 ✉ Obala Bana Berislavića 22
☎ 021 885 400; www.concordia-hotel.net

VIS

San Giorgio ££
This delightful, family-run hotel in the Old Town of Vis has tastefully designed modern rooms and a welcoming restaurant. The hotel also has its own wine cellar and shop with wine-tasting.
✚ 203 D1 ✉ Ul. Petra Hektorovića 2, Vis
☎ 021 711 362; www.hotelsangiorgiovis.com

Where to ...
Eat and Drink

Prices
Expect to pay for a starter, main course, salad and house wine or water for one:
£ under 100kn   **££** 100kn–200kn   **£££** over 200kn

BRAČ

Konoba Marija ££

Insider Tip

This must have the most perfect location of just about any restaurant in Croatia – high up on a terrace with views over the pine woods and the sea to the island of Hvar. You can get there by walking or cycling the 4km (2.5-mile) track from Bol along the cliffs to the wine village of Murvica; it is, however, also possible to drive. Meat and fish are barbecued on an open fire – try the Brač lamb or the mixed grill for two, perhaps accompanied by a jug of wine from the local vineyards. A nice touch is the basket of garlic bread, toasted on the grill and brought to the table with your meal.

➕ 203 F2 ✉ Murvica, near Bol
🕐 Apr–Sep daily 10am–midnight

Palute £

Popular Palute is right on the waterfront in Supetar, close to where the ferries come in from Split. The menu has a wide selection of grilled meat and fish dishes at reasonable prices. Fans of good, traditional food go for the sheep's cheese followed by grilled lamb and side dishes. The family also runs a comfortable bed-and-breakfast a short walk from the port.

➕ 203 F3 ✉ Porat 4, Supetar
☎ 021 631 730 🕐 Daily 10am–11pm

HVAR

Eremitaž ££

Located not far from little St Jerolim's Church to the north of Stari Grad, right on the water, this long-estab-

lished restaurant offers guests quality Dalmatian cuisine in a romantic setting. Of all the delicacies on the menu the fish platter could not be fresher and is really outstanding. In autumn, game such as wild boar goulash is served. For dessert, try the figs in choux pastry with an orange and honey sauce.

➕ 203 E2 ✉ Put Rudine 2, Stari Grad ☎ 021 766 167 🕐 Jun–Sep daily noon–3, 6–midnight

Konoba Menego ££

Dine by candlelight or eat outside with a wine barrel for a table at this family-run tavern in an old stone house on the steps leading up from the harbour to the castle. Everything here is home-made or produced locally, from wine from the Pakleni Islands to Hvar goat's cheese with honey. The mixed meat and fish platter is generous indeed and the choice of vegetarian dishes exemplary. For pudding, try the 'drunken figs' stuffed with almonds and soaked in brandy – said to be an ancient aphrodisiac, followed by Turkish coffee with walnut or wild orange liqueur. The Kovačević family also own a vineyard and have a summer restaurant on the nearby island of Sveti Kliment.

➕ 203 E2 ✉ Groda, Hvar Town
☎ 021 742 036 🕐 Apr–Oct daily noon–2, 5–11

Luna ££

Luna is one of a quartet of trendy restaurants on the same street, just a flight of steps up from the main square. This chic trattoria features Italian and Mediterranean cuisine, from fresh pasta dishes and steak with truffles to gazpacho, salads and fish stew with potatoes and white wine. On warm evenings you can dine on the roof terrace.

➕ 203 E2 ✉ Ulica Petra Hektorovića 5, Hvar Town ☎ 021 741 400
🕐 Apr–Oct daily noon–midnight

Zlatna Školjka £££

In Hvar's trendy restaurant quarter, the 'Golden Shell' advertises 'slow food', using local ingredients and inventive takes on traditional dishes, such as goat's cheese in olive oil, gnocchi with almonds, beef stuffed with goat's cheese or rabbit with figs. Booking is advised, especially in the months of July and August.

➕ 203 E2 ✉ Ulica Petra Hektorovića 8, Hvar Town ☎ 098 1 688 797
🕐 Summer daily noon–3, 7–midnight

SPLIT

Kod Jože ££

Hidden away in an old stone house on a quiet lane near Strossmayerov Park, this excellent *konoba* (tavern) serves first-class meat and fish dishes. The speciality here is fresh fish, including sea bass, John Dory, lobster and squid, but the menu also features frogs' legs in bread-crumbs, grilled vegetables and unusual offerings such as mangold risotto. There is a good selection of steaks, including one stuffed with Dalmatian ham and cheese. You can eat outside on a shady terrace, or inside which is decorated in a traditional style, with old wine barrels and fishing nets.

➕ 203 E3 ✉ Ulica Sredmanuška 4
☎ 021 347 397 🕐 Mon–Fri 9am–midnight, Sat–Sun noon–midnight

TROGIR

Konoba Škrapa £

The back streets of Trogir offer a wide choice of restaurants, many with attractive courtyards and sum-mer gardens, but for no-nonsense, simple Dalmatian food, it's hard to beat Škrapa. It's best to stick to the basics here, like plates of ham or steaming bowls of *fažol* (bean stew). The atmosphere is hectic and the table decoration eccentric, but a meal here is great fun and you won't find better value for money anywhere.

Insider Tip

➕ 203 E3 ✉ Ulica Hrvatskih Mučenika 9
☎ 021 885 313 🕐 Mon–Sat 11–11, Sun 4–11

VIS

Lola £££

Visitors to this enchanting restaurant in Vis Town will be surprised by its romantic garden hidden behind high walls right in the middle of the town. Imaginatively furnished in a vintage style, this alone is a refreshing change from perpetually being surrounded by maritime knick-knacks. The food is based on Dalmatian recipes but comple-mented by modern trends including sushi, tapas and burgers. Emphasis is placed on regional products – Lola even has its own vegetable garden on the mainland. After dining, the restaurant turns into a relaxed bar with DJs playing lounge music in the summer.

➕ 203 D1 ✉ Matije Gupca 12, Vis town
☎ 095 8 497 932; www.lolavisisland.com
🕐 summer 8am–midnight

Villa Kaliopa £££

During the summer, the harbour at Vis fills up with yachts and many owners come ashore to dine in this exclusive and romantic restaurant, with fountains and statues in the walled garden of a 16th-century villa. The menu focuses on fresh seafood and changes according to what is available locally at the market. The waiter will recommend the best dishes of the day. If you need to know the prices then you probably can't afford to eat here!

➕ 203 D1 ✉ Ulica Vladimira Nazora 32, Vis town ☎ 091 2 711 755
🕐 Summer daily 5–midnight

Where to ...
Shop

The best shopping is in the towns of Split, Šibenik, Trogir and Zadar. Hvar Town has a number of fashionable boutiques. On top of this, each of the islands has its own speciality – lavender in Hvar, marble in Brač, wine in Vis.

HVAR AND VIS

Wherever you go on Hvar in summer you will find street stalls offering **lavender** in various forms – as dried flowers, oil or soap.

A more unusual souvenir from Hvar is **lace** made from the agave plant; it is produced exclusively by the Benedictine nuns in Hvar Town, using a technique imported from the Canary Islands.

In both Hvar and Vis, you will come across cellars selling the local wine. Look out for the delicious dry white Vugava and the red Viški Plavac.

SPLIT

Most of the shops in Split are concentrated on the busy pedestrian streets of the medieval town, set back from the waterfront.

The main thoroughfare is **Marmontova**, where several trendy boutiques sell women's fashions and shoes, including reasonably priced imported Italian designer brands.

The stalls in the underground galleries of **Diocletian's Palace** sell arts, crafts and cheap souvenirs.

Split's main market, **Pazar**, outside the eastern gate of the palace, sells a wide range of items.

Where to ...
Go Out

Entertainment on the Dalmatian islands and coast takes many forms, from windsurfing, scuba diving and river-rafting to drinking at waterfront bars.

MUSIC AND DRAMA

There are many cultural festivals in summer, with concerts and performances in local churches and open-air venues in July and August. Look out for recitals of medieval, Baroque and chamber music in **St Donat's Church** in Zadar, concerts in **Trogir Cathedral** and in the courtyard of **Kamerlengo Fort**.

In Split, performances of opera, ballet and plays take place throughout the year at the **Hrvatsko Narodno Kazalište** (Croatian National Theatre) on Trg Gaje Bulata (tel: 021 344 399; www.hnk-split.hr), but the big event is the **Split Summer Festival** (www.splitsko-ljeto.hr). For four weeks in July and August, the peristyle of Diocletian's Palace becomes an open-air stage; the highlight is the performance of a Verdi opera.

In Hvar Town, performances held at the **Hvarsko Kazalište** are a highlight. At the time of going to press, however, this venue was closed for renovation.

Performances of classical and modern drama take place throughout the summer when there are also evening concerts in the nearby Franciscan monastery. **Carpe Diem** in Hvar is one of the best-known beach clubs in Croatia (www.carpe-diem-hvar.com).

Dubrovnik and South Dalmatia

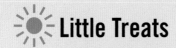 **Little Treats**

An unforgettable boat trip
Ferries to the **Elaphiti Islands** (➤ 162) transport everything from sacks of mail, fridges, crates of drinks and live animals – and of course holiday-makers.

Korzo à la Dubrovnik
Just before the sun sets, make yourself look your best and join the promenade up and down the **Stradun** (➤ 153). Quite a spectacle!

Adriatic sundowner
Sneak through a gap in **Dubrovnik's town wall** (➤ 153) and enjoy a refreshing drink on the cliffs at the Buža Bar!

Getting Your Bearings

The southern Dalmatian coastline is dominated by Dubrovnik, a perfectly preserved walled town described by the English poet Lord Byron (1788–1824) quite rightly as the 'pearl of the Adriatic'.

While much of Dalmatia was ruled by Venice, Dubrovnik was the centre of the powerful city-state of Ragusa for 450 years, paying notional tribute to Ottoman sultans and Hungarian kings while refusing to be ruled by either. During its golden age in the 15th and 16th centuries, the city grew rich from shipping and was known as the 'Croatian Athens', a melting pot of cultures and a meeting place for the greatest artists, scientists, cartographers and explorers of the day. It was during this time that the city walls were built and a walk around the walls

TOP 10

⭐ Dubrovnik ➤ 152
⭐ Korčula ➤ 156

Don't Miss

50 Mljet ➤ 159

At Your Leisure

51 Lastovo ➤ 161
52 Pelješac ➤ 161
53 Trsteno ➤ 162
54 Elafitski Otoci
   (Elafiti ilands) ➤ 162
55 Lokrum ➤ 163
56 Cavtat ➤ 163

still provides one of the most memorable experiences of any visit to Croatia.

After suffering extensive damage during the siege of 1991–92, Dubrovnik has been brilliantly restored and once again has the feel of a lively open-air museum, with churches, palaces, cafés and narrow streets paved in marble.

Dubrovnik makes a good base for visiting the rest of southern Dalmatia – from the unspoiled islands of Mljet, Lopud and Šipan to the vineyards of the Pelješac peninsula and mini-Dubrovnik, Korčula. North of Dubrovnik, the Magistrala coastal highway passes through a short section of Bosnia-Hercegovina (passports required) on its way to the Neretva delta where much of Croatia's citrus fruit is grown. To the south, beyond the pretty resort of Cavtat, the fertile Konavle valley squeezes between the mountains of Bosnia and Montenegro.

left: Small fishing boats moored in Cavtat

right: Dubrovnik's fortifications

Three Perfect Days

If you're not quite sure where to begin your trip, this itinerary recommends a practical and enjoyable three-day tour of Dubrovnik and South Dalmatia. For more information see the main entries (► 152).

Day 1

Morning
Stroll around the narrow streets in the Old Town of ⭐**Dubrovnik** (left, ► 152) that lie both sides of the main street, Stradun. Afterwards, relax with a coffee on the terrace of Gradskavana before a seafood lunch by the harbour at Lokanda Peskarija (► 166).

Afternoon and evening
Take a stroll around Dubrovnik's town walls, gazing down over the rooftops and out to sea. The ticket for the walls also gives access to Lovrijenac, beyond Pile Gate. Climb the steps to the fortress for a wonderful view at sunset then have dinner at Orhan (► 166), overlooking a peaceful cove in the shadow of the fort.

Day 2

Morning and afternoon
Go down to the harbour in Gruž to catch the *Nona Ana* catamaran that leaves daily at 9am in summer (10am in winter) for 🌀**Mljet** (► 159). This gives you six hours on the island, enough time to explore the Mljet National Park on foot or by bike and take a boat to St Mary's, a 12th-century Benedictine monastery on an islet in the middle of a lake.

Evening
Spend your second evening in Dubrovnik inside the Old Town which gets particularly lively on

summer evenings. If you can, take in a performance during the Summer Festival (► 168); otherwise, have dinner at **Gil's little Bistro** (► 166) then head
to the **Troubadour Café** where live jazz is performed at around
10pm most nights.

Day 3

Morning
Head north along the Magistrala coast road, pausing to walk around the
botanical garden in **53 Trsteno** (► 162) before continuing to **52 Pelješac**
penninsula (► 161). After a lunch of local oysters next to the harbour at
Mali Ston, you can walk off your meal with a circuit of the walls at nearby
Veli Ston.

Afternoon and evening
Drive across the Pelješac peninsula, perhaps stopping to taste or buy
wine at the Dingač vineyards in Potomje. Arrive at Orebić in time to
make the short ferry crossing to ★ **8 Korčula** (below, ► 156). Spend the
evening walking around Korčula and having dinner on the sea wall at
Morski Konjic (► 167).

Dubrovnik

Dubrovnik is the jewel in Croatia's crown – a beautifully restored town, full of Gothic and Renaissance architecture, crowded onto a rocky headland and surrounded by its 15th-century walls.

From 1358 to 1808 this was the Republic of Ragusa, one of the wealthiest places in Europe, whose merchant fleet was reputed to be the third largest in the world. Much of the town was rebuilt following an earthquake in 1667. The especially elegant appearance of Dubrovnik's main thoroughfare, Stradun, is thanks to the strict specifications and uniform architectural style chosen when rebuilding the town at that time.

During the siege of 1991–92, bombardments by the Serbs damaged more than 70 percent of the buildings in the Old Town. Walking around Dubrovnik today, there are few signs of the recent war and the maps at the entrance gates, pin-pointing the damage in detail, come as quite a shock. The town has recovered its confidence, the tourists have returned and there is a buzz in the air around the outdoor cafés once again.

Getting there

The pedestrianised Old Town is eminently walkable. The best entrance is through **Pile Gate** (Vrata od Pile), where most local buses stop. Cross the stone bridge and wooden drawbridge to reach the outer gate. Above the archway is a figure of St Blaise, a 3rd-century bishop from Armenia who

Following its comprehensive renovation, Dubrovnik's Old Town has regained its former glory

★ A WALK AROUND THE WALLS
The high point of any visit to Dubrovnik is a walk around the town walls that are up to 25m (82ft) high and 6m (19ft) thick in places, reinforced with bastions and towers. The complete circuit is about 2km (1.2mi) and takes at least an hour, looking down over courtyards, gardens and restored rooftops, as well as giving superb views out to sea and to the little island of Lokrum. For the finest views, climb up to the roof of the Tvrđava Minčeta, designed by Michelozzo Michelozzi of Florence in 1455. The best place to begin a circuit of the walls that children find equally thrilling is just inside Pile Gate, though the walls can also be accessed from Ploče Gate and Tvrđava Sv. Ivana. The walls are open from Jun–Aug daily 8–7, Apr, May and Sep 8–6:30, Oct 8–5:30 and Nov–Mar 9–3, 100kn.

was martyred by the Romans and became the patron saint of Dubrovnik after he appeared in a dream to a priest, warning of a Venetian attack. The Pile Gate leads straight into Stradun, the Old Town's principal street. The other main entrance is **Ploče Gate** (Vrata od Ploče) which is on the eastern side of the town.

Stradun

The best-known avenue in Croatia is both a busy shopping street and the venue for the *korzo* or evening promenade. Once lined with palaces, it was rebuilt after the earthquake in a uniform style. Since then, its houses and shopfronts all have arched doorways at ground-floor level and pretty green-shuttered window-frames above.

At the eastern-most end, beneath the clock tower, Stradun broadens out into **Luža Square**, with the **Orlando Column** (► 184) in the middle. The southern side of the square is closed off by the **Church of St Blaise** (Sv. Vlaha), with an altar containing a 15th-century gilded statue of the saint; opposite the church is **Sponza Palace**, Ragusa's former customs house in a typical mixture of styles ranging from Gothic to Renaissance. It is a rare survivor of the earthquake.

Franjevački Samostan

If you enter the town through Pile Gate, you will immediately come across a **Franciscan monastery** from the 14th century. It boasts a beautiful cloisters and a 15th-century wooden portrait of St Blaise that hangs in the monastery museum. Near the cloisters is a dispensary dating from 1317, said to be the oldest continuously operating pharmacy in Europe.

Dominikanski Samostan

This 15th-century Dominican monastery church is reached by a grand staircase inside **Ploče Gate**. The highlight is the delightful cloister of orange trees. The monastery museum contains a painting of Mary Magdalene by Titian (c. 1488–1576) and the church features a Virgin and Child by Ivan Meštrović (1883–1962).

Katedrala

Dubrovnik's Baroque cathedral was completed in 1713, replacing an earlier church destroyed in the earthquake. The white walls give it a feeling of light and space, in contrast to the treasury behind the altar. This collection features rich gold and silver filigree work, including macabre objects, designed by local artists. Among items on display is a skull case for the head of St Blaise and a 16th-century casket said to contain Jesus' swaddling clothes.

In the Old Town of Dubrovnik

Knežev Dvor

Dubrovnik's municipal museum is housed in the **Rector's Palace**, the former seat of government of the Ragusan Republic. First built between 1435 and 1461, it was rebuilt exactly as before after the earthquake in 1667. It was here the the *Knez* (rector) would spend his entire but brief term of office of just one month. A tour takes in the state apartments that are filled with antique furniture and the former dungeons. During the **Summer Festival**, classical concerts are held in the museum's courtyard.

➕ 205 E1

Tourist Information Office
➕ 212 A3 ✉ Brsalje 5 ☎ 020 312 011; www.tzdubrovnik.hr

Franjevački Samostan
➕ 212 A3 ✉ Stradun 2 🕐 Daily 9–6 💰 30kn

Dominikanski Samostan
➕ 212 C2 ✉ Ulica Svetog Dominika 🕐 Daily 9–6 💰 20kn

Katedrala
➕ 212 B/C2 ✉ Pred Dvorom 🕐 Summer Mon–Sat 9–5, Sun 11–5, winter Mon–Sat 8–5, Sun 11–5 💰 Treasury 15kn

Knežev Dvor
➕ 212 C2 ✉ Pred Dvorom 🕐 May–Oct daily 9–18, Nov–Apr Mon–Sat 9–4 💰 70kn

INSIDER INFO

- Dubrovnik's **town beach** is at Banje, beyond Ploče Gate, a broad sweep of pebbles with views to the Old Town. A section is reserved for the extremely elegant **East West Beach Club** with its stylish loungers, restaurant, bar and nightclub. A popular place to swim and sunbathe is the offshore island of **Lokrum** (ferries leave from the old harbour).
- The **Sinagoga** (Synagogue) on Ulica Žudioska serves Dubrovnik's small Jewish community, one of the earliest Sephardic congregations in the world, following their expulsion from Spain in 1492. Among the items on display in the museum is a list of earthquake victims from 1667 and a memorial to 27 Dubrovnik Jews who were murdered during the Holocaust.

 Korčula

The town stands proudly on a peninsula and its Venetian walls make it look like a miniature version of Dubrovnik. The island that gave the town its name is one of the greenest in the Adriatic, with cypress and pine woods and vineyards that were planted by the ancient Greeks.

Insider Tip

The easiest way of getting to Korčula from southern Dalmatia is on a regular ferry from Orebić on the Pelješac peninsula. The car ferry docks at **Dominče**, 2km (1.2mi) south of Korčula town; if you are touring without a car, there is a passenger ferry which comes in right on the harbour in Korčula itself. The main coastal ferry from Rijeka to Dubrovnik calls in at Korčula and there are also ferries and catamarans from Split to Vela Luka, the island's main town, 45km (28mi) from Korčula at its western tip. There is also a fast catamaran connection between Dubrovnik and Korčula.

Strolling around the Old Town

Korčula is a compact town, huddled onto a narrow peninsula and still largely enclosed by its medieval walls and round towers. The Old Town is perfect for walking and a stroll around the outer walls along a pine-shaded promenade takes all of 15 minutes. From here, there are views to the mountains of the Pelješac peninsula, just 2km (1.2mi) away. The main entry to the Old Town is through the **Land Gate** (Kopnena Vrata), reached by a broad flight of steps leading up to Revelin Tower. Above the arch is a relief of the winged lion of St Mark, the symbol of Venice. The 15th-century tower has been restored to house a permanent exhibition on **Moreška sword dancers**, who can be seen performing nearby twice a week in summer (daily 9–9, winter 10–6, 20kn) (➤ 28f).

Insider Tip

A passenger ferry moored in the harbour at Korčula

From here, a single street runs the length of the Old Town, with narrow lanes dropping down to the sea on either side. Almost immediately you reach the tiny main square, dominated by the **St Mark's Cathedral**, begun in the 13th century and completed over the next

300 years in a mixture of Gothic and Renaissance styles.

The cathedral **Treasury** (open summer daily 10–1, 5–7, 20Kn) houses an eclectic collection of artworks, from a 15th-century altarpiece to a naïve *Annunciation* by a local artist Ana Fištanic. The Town Museum (open Jul–Aug daily 9–9, Apr–Jun and Sep–Oct 9–2, 20kn) is housed in a 16th-century palace across the square. Near here is **Marco Polo's House**, said to be the birthplace of the Venetian traveller Marco Polo (1254–1324). In the summer you can climb the tower for a beautiful view; there are plans to open a Marco Polo museum here (summer daily 9–9, rest of the year 10–2, 20kn).

TAKING A BREAK

The **Massimo cocktail bar** (open May–Oct daily 6pm–2am, ££) on Šetalište Petra Kanavelića makes a great place for a sunset apéritif on the sea walls.

➕ 204 B2

Tourist Information Office
✉ Obala Franje Tuđmana
☎ 020 715 701; www.visitkorcula.eu

Land Gate (Kopnena Vrata) is the main entrance into the Old Town

INSIDER INFO

- A performance of the 🎭 **Moreška sword dance** is well worth seeing. Spirited displays are given at festivals and on Monday and Thursday evenings throughout the summer – and are much loved by children too.
- Taste the island's **white wine** while you are here! Not just Grk from Lumbarda but also Pošip and Rukatac are delicious.
- Take a water-taxi in summer to the **island of Badija** that has several good pebbly beaches, including one for nudists. Alternatively, take a bus or boat trip to the **wine village of Lumbarda**, 6km (4mi) from Korčula, where you can walk through the vineyards to the beautiful sandy beach at **Prižna**.
- The **Icon Museum** (summer daily 10–1, 6–8, low season 9–2, 20kn), in a narrow lane off Šetalište Petra Kanavelića, contains a collection of Cretan Orthodox icons, looted by Venetian troops in battles with the Ottoman Empire. A stone bridge leads from the museum to noteworthy **All Saints' Church**, with a carved wooden altarpiece beneath a 15th-century canopy.

50 Mljet

The southernmost of Croatia's major islands is a beautiful and unspoiled place of pine and oak woods, steep cliffs, saltwater lakes and coves.

Mljet island is now a national park

Mljet is 37km (23mi) long and just 3km (2mi) wide. It has a mythical appeal for Croatians, as the legendary home of the nymph Calypso who is said to have seduced Ulysses and held him captive for seven years in her cave on the south coast after he was shipwrecked on the island. If you would like to read more about it, Homer relates the myth in the fifth book of his *Odyssey*.

Mljet National Park

Most people visit the **Nacionalni Park Mljet** that covers 31sq km (12 sqmi) of forest and lakes on the west of the island, on day trips. The easiest way to get there is on the daily catamaran *Nona Ana* which makes the journey from Dubrovnik in under two hours. Tickets are on sale from 8am each morning on the quayside in Gruž. From June to September the boat takes you to **Polače**, inside the national park, allowing you six hours on the island; at other times, when the boat drops you at Sobra, you will probably need to stay overnight. In summer, you can also visit Mljet on organised excursions from Dubrovnik, Cavtat, Korčula and Orebić, with the entry fee to the national park included in the price.

Insider Tip

Dubrovnik and South Dalmatia

Exploring Mljet

Arriving at **Polače**, you can buy a ticket and pick up a map from the kiosk by the harbour. The ticket includes a mini-bus transfer to the park headquarters at Pristanište, but it is just as pleasant to walk on the well-marked path beginning behind the ruins of a 4th-century Roman palace. This brings you out by the shore of **Veliko Jezero**, the larger of two saltwater lakes connected to the sea by a narrow channel. A footpath leads around the two lakes which meet at Stari Most (Old Bridge), where you can rent bicycles, canoes and rowing boats in summer.

A bird's-eye view of the jagged island of Mljet

The ticket also includes a boat transfer from Pristanište or Stari Most to **St Mary's Island** where you will find one of Croatia's most photographed sights – a 12th-century **Benedictine monastery** – on an islet in the middle of the lake. Used as a hotel during the Yugoslav era, the monastery is now in a poor state of repair, but it is still an atmospheric place.

TAKING A BREAK

There are several cafés and restaurants on the **seafront at Polače**, a summer restaurant on **St Mary's Island** and another, **Mali Ra**j, on the shores of Veliko Jezero.

✚ 204 C1

Nacionalni Park Mljet
✉ Pristanište 2
☎ 020 744 058; www.np-mljet.hr
💶 90–100kn

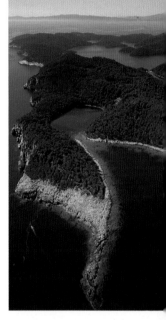

INSIDER INFO

- Climb to the summit of **Montokuc** (253m/830ft), the highest point in the national park, for a view over the island. The path is signposted from the shores of Veliko Jezero, near Pristanište.
- Although most people visit on day trips, it is possible to stay on the island. There is a **hotel at Pomena** (► 165) and several places on the waterfront at Polače have rooms. **Saplunara**, on the southern tip of Mljet, has one of Dalmatia's finest sandy beaches; although the village is almost deserted, local families rent out rooms here and set up fish restaurants in summer.

At Your Leisure

51 Lastovo

Like Istria, this island south of Korčula belonged to Italy between the two world wars. From 1976 to 1989 no foreigners were allowed to visit it. Over the past few years it has evolved into a hip tourist destination for sailing enthusiasts and individual tourists. The island is connected to the mainland by a ferry from Split that operates every day. In the summer, a fast catamaran service runs from Dubrovnik via Mljet to Korčula and on to Lastovo. Boats arrive in Ubli harbour. The little port is 10 km (6.4 mi) from Lastovo, the largest settlement on the island.

With a population of under 1000, Lastovo feels like a place apart and there is little to do but walk in the fertile countryside, swim from secluded beaches and take boat trips in summer to the uninhabited islets of the archipelago.

Insider Tip

On Shrove Tuesday each year, the island plays host to one of Croatia's strangest **Carnival celebrations**, when a straw figure known as **Poklad** is paraded through town on a donkey before being ritually burned while dancers perform a local variation of the **Korčula sword dance**.

➕ 204 B1

Tourist Information Office
✉ Lastovo town ☎ 020 801 018, www.tz-lastovo.hr

52 Pelješac

This long mountainous finger of land is effectively an island, known throughout Croatia for its expensive Dingač and Postup red wines. A single road runs the 90km (56-mile) length of the peninsula, with views across to the islands of Korčula, Lastovo, Mljet, Hvar and Vis from beaches on the west coast.

The twin towns of **Mali Ston** and **Ston** guard the entrance to the peninsula, fortified by 14th-century walls which once formed the second longest defensive system in the world after the Great Wall of China. You can walk on the wall

Vineyards on the Pelješac peninsula

PELJEŠAC WINES

You can taste and buy local wines at the **Dingač and Matuško Vina wineries** in the village of **Potomje**. The best red wine, Dingač, is produced from Plavac Mali grapes grown on the southern, sea-facing slopes.

- **Dingač** (tel: 020 742 010).
- **Matuško Vina** (tel: 020 742 399).

Šipan harbour

itself at Ston; the section from here to Mali Ston has been recently restored. From Ston, the road passes through the vineyards at **Potomje**, the centre of the Dingač wine producing area, on its way to the pleasant beach resort of **Orebić**, 2km (1.2mi) from Korčula across a narrow channel.

✚ 198 A2

Tourist Information Office
✉ Zrinsko Frankopanska 2, Orebić
☎ 020 713 718; www.visitorebic-croatia

53 Trsteno

The 16th-century aristocrat Ivan Gučetić built his summer villa in the seaside village of Trsteno, where leading poets, artists and statesmen from the Republic of Ragusa would gather to discuss politics and stroll in the elegant gardens overlooking the sea. The house and garden remained in the Gučetić family until 1947.

Now an **arboretum**, the gardens make a lovely place to walk, with shady avenues, hedges and exotic trees, many grown from seeds brought back by local sailors from their travels. The highlight is the **ornamental fishpond**, just behind the villa, where a figure of Neptune with his trident stands guard over a grotto, flanked by a pair of nymphs.

The gardens were badly damaged by fire caused by shelling in 1991, but fortunately they have recovered well. A steep path leads down to Trsteno's harbour, with views of the Elafiti Islands offshore.

✚ 205 E2   ☎ 020 751 019
🕐 Summer daily 7–7, winter 8–6   🎟 35kn

54 Elafitski Otoci

The tiny Elafiti islands of **Koločep**, **Lopud** and **Šipan** provide peaceful havens just a short ferry ride away from the bustle of Dubrovnik.

During the golden age of Ragusa, many Dubrovnik nobles built their summer houses here and the islands are still a popular weekend retreat. Several Renaissance villas on Šipan that are not unlike small fortresses have been well preserved. There are regular ferries to the Elafiti Islands from the harbour at **Gruž**, with additional excursion boats from Dubrovnik's old port in summer. Children in particular like the old **Jadrolinija ferries**, on which everything imaginable is transported to the islands, including chickens.

With orchards, vegetable gardens, vineyards, pine woods, ancient

At Your Leisure

FOLKLORE AND COSTUMES
Cavtat is the main town of the Konavle region, a narrow strip of land between Dubrovnik and the Montenegro border. The area is known for its inhabitants' **folk costumes** that can be seen every Sunday morning in summer in the village of **Čilipi** when **folklore performances** and **traditional courtship dances** are put on for tourists in front of the church.

Insider Tip

stone chapels and churches, fishing villages, quiet beaches and fewer than 1000 permanent residents, the islands have a relaxed, laid-back charm. Hike through the countryside, discover the quiet little harbours or dive into the water in a remote bay – but be careful. Don't get too carried away and forget the times of the last ferry. The best 🏊 **sandy beach** is on Lopud near Šunj.
➕ 205 D2

55 Lokrum
Just 15 minutes by boat from Dubrovnik, the wooded isle of Lokrum makes a popular half-day outing (► 186). The English king Richard the Lionheart (1157–99) is said to have been shipwrecked here on his way back from the Crusades, while in the 19th century the island was a summer retreat for Archduke Maximilian of Habsburg, the younger brother of the Austro-Hungarian emperor Franz Josef I, who converted the old **Benedictine monastery** into a private villa and laid out the formal gardens that can be visited today.

There is good swimming here, both in the warm, shallow saltwater lake known as the 🏊 **Mrtvo More** (Dead Sea) and from the spectacularly sited nudist beach on the east side of the island, signposted from the jetty. Boats depart regularly for Lokrum in summer from the old harbour at Dubrovnik (from 9am, last return 6pm, 50kn) in winter, there are also occasional weekend excursions, or you can find a taxi-boat to take you.
➕ 205 E1

56 Cavtat
Cavtat is less than 20km (12mi) south of Dubrovnik and only a few minutes from the airport. It is one of Croatia's prettiest resorts, set around a horseshoe bay and surrounded by sandy beaches. The painter **Vlaho Bukovac** (1855–1922) was born here and you can visit his house and studio near the waterfront; his image of 19th-century Cavtat harbour can be seen above the chancel in the nearby **Church of Our Lady of the Snows**. A path from here leads to the summit of the **Rat peninsula** where the Greek city of Epidauros once stood. Founded in the 4th century BC, it was taken by the Romans one century later and abandoned in the 7th century after being captured by the Avars and Slavs. The inhabitants fled to the north and founded Dubrovnik. The dome-shaped Račić Mausoleum on the same site was created by Ivan Meštrović for a rich shipping family from Cavtat.

With cafés on the palm-lined promenade and 5km (3mi) of seafront paths linking beaches and pine woods, Cavtat makes a good base for a relaxing family holiday by the seaside. There are a number of boats which depart regularly throughout the summer months for the old harbour in Dubrovnik.
➕ 205 E1
🚌 Bus 10 from Dubrovnik

Tourist Information Office
✉ Tiha 3
☎ 020 479 025,
http://visit-konavle.com

Where to ...
Stay

Prices
Expect to pay per person per night for a double room in summer:
£ under 300kn   ££ 300kn–600kn   £££ over 600kn

CAVTAT

Supetar £££
This small, attractive hotel is set in an old stone house on the water-front, with lovely views across the bay to the Sustjepan Peninsula. It is just a short distance from a pebbly beach and concrete bathing platform, though guests also have access to the swimming pool at Hotel Croatia, a large, luxury, five-star hotel belonging to the same company on the other side of the bay. Hotel Croatia is only a few minutes walk away from the cafés and restaurants of the seafront promenade where boats depart regularly for Dubrovnik.

➕ 205 E1 ✉ ObalaA. Starčevića 27
☎ 020 479 833; www.adrialicluxuryhotels.com
🕐 Apr–Oct

DUBROVNIK

There are only a handfull of small hotels in the Old Town of Dubrovnik. Most of the top hotels are outside Ploče Gate, while the majority of package accommodation is on the Lapad and Babin Kuk peninsulas, 5km (3mi) west of the town, or in the resorts of Cavtat, Mlini and Plat to the south.

Grand Villa Argentina £££
The guest list at the Argentina has included Tito, Margaret Thatcher, Richard Burton and Elizabeth Taylor. The hotel, traditionally considered the top address in town,

is made up of four separate villas, including the lovely Villa Orsula from the 1930s and the early 20th-century folly Villa Sheherazade, as well as a modern building. Steps lead down through the gardens to a small private beach; there are also outdoor seawater and heated indoor pools. The sea-facing rooms have views to the Old Town, a 10-minute walk away.

➕ 212 off C3 ✉ Frana Supila 14
☎ 020 440 555; www.adrialicluxuryhotels.com

Old Town Hostel £
This hostel in the heart of the Old Town offers bright, cheerfully furnished dormitory accommodation as well as rooms with two and three beds, many with their own shower and WC. Some rooms even have their own tiny balcony. Communal kitchen and terrace, free Internet access and Skype, breakfast around the clock and a very helpful staff are additional plus points in this hostel that is especially popular among younger holiday-makers.

➕ 212 B3 ✉ Od Sigurate 7
☎ 020 007 322,
www.dubrovnikoldtownhostel.com

Pucić Palace £££
This five-star boutique hotel is housed in an 18th-century palace not far from the market square in the Old Town. It's a gem of a place with an atmosphere of informal luxury that set a trend for small town-house hotels in Croatia. The 19 rooms have original artworks, antique furniture, hand-

woven rugs and dark oak parquet floors, along with modern conveniences such as DVD players and satellite TV. Dining options include a boulevard café, wine bar and terrace restaurant (summer only) serving Middle Eastern cuisine. A private yacht is also available for guests to rent.

➕ 212 B2 ✉ Ulica Od Puča 1 ☎ 020 326 200; www.thepucicpalace.com

Stari Grad £££

The only other place to stay within the Old Town walls is this small hotel, with just eight rooms, in an old mansion close to Pile Gate. Its old mirrors, chandeliers, antique furnishings and rugs lend it a great deal of charm.

Insider Tip A highlight is the small roof terrace, with magnificent views over the town.

➕ 212 B3 ✉ Od Sigurate 4 ☎ 020 322 244; www.hotelstarigrad.com

Vila Curić ££

These 14 modern self-catering apartments are in a quiet street on the Babin Kuk peninsula, overlooking Gruž harbour and the Rijeka Dubrovačka bridge. All with a kitchen, bathroom and living-room. Some have a balcony or terrace. The beaches and promenades of Babin Kuk are close by and the Old Town is a bus ride away, making this a good place to combine a seaside holiday with a town break.

➕ 212 off A3 ✉ Ulica Mostarska 2 ☎ 020 436 555; www.vila-curic.hr 🚌 Bus 6

Villa Dubrovnik £££

This low-rise white Modernist villa, hidden among fragrant gardens filled with orange and lemon trees, has long been the most romantic place to stay in Dubrovnik. Steps lead down to a private beach and the cliffside terraces have views of Lokrum and the Old Port – just a short boat trip away on the hotel's private shuttle. Originally built as a rest home for Socialist officials and used to house refugees and soldiers during the Croatian War of Independence, the hotel is showing its age. It closed in 2007 for renovation, completed in the summer of 2009.

➕ 212 off C3 ✉ Ulica Vlaha Bukovca 6 ☎ 020 500 300; www.villa-dubrovnik.hr 🕐 Apr–Oct

KORČULA

Korčula ££

The large package hotels are all on the fringes of Korčula town, but if you want to be more central and don't mind dated rooms, the best choice is the Korčula. With 20 rooms in a white stone building dating from 1912, it stands just outside the town walls, next to one of the entrances to the Old Town. Be sure to have an evening drink on the west-facing waterfront terrace which is perfectly placed to catch the sunset and has views across to the Pelješac peninsula.

➕ 204 B2 ✉ Obala Franje Tuđmana 5, Korčula town ☎ 020 711 078; www.htp-korcula.hr

MLJET

Odisej ££

The only large hotel on the island is inside Mljet National Park, next to a small cove in the pretty seaside village of Pomena. The 156 rooms are spread out in a number of whitewashed pavilions and there are also two apartments (£££) that have their own kitchenette, living-room and balcony with sea view. This is a good base for an active holiday, with scuba diving and sailing courses on offer and bicycles for rent. A short walk from Pomena leads through the woods to Malo Jezero, a small saltwater lake.

➕ 204 B2 ✉ Pomena ☎ 020 362 111, www.adriaticluxuryhotels.com 🕐 Apr–Oct

Where to ...
Eat and Drink

Prices

Expect to pay for a starter, main course, salad and house wine or water for one:

£ under 100kn   ££ 100kn–200kn   £££ over 200kn

CAVTAT

Galija £££

This old-style tavern and wine cellar is on a cobbled street leading uphill towards the cemetery. You can eat indoors in winter, but the main attraction on summer evenings is the beautiful seaside terrace, with tables set with candles and fine linen beneath the pine trees. The Dalmatian food and wine are first-class, from the free starter of fish pâté to smoked ham, seafood risotto, boiled sea bass, grilled fish and barbecued steaks. More inventive dishes might include sea urchins, shrimps in honey or carpaccio of grouper with parmesan and rocket (arugula), an excellent choice for a celebration meal.

➕ 205 E1 ✉ Vuličevićeva 1
☎ 020 478 566
🕙 Daily 11am–midnight

DUBROVNIK

Buffet Škola £

The tiny Buffet Škola, just off the Stradun, makes the best sandwiches in town. Nothing fancy, just thick slices of crusty home-made bread filled with Dalmatian ham or cheese with oil and tomato. You can find it at the foot of a narrow alley leading up towards Prijeko. In summer there are also a couple of tables out on the street for eating alfresco.

➕ 212 B2 ✉ Antuninska 1
☎ 020 321 096
🕙 Daily 8am–midnight

Gil's little Bistro £££

Gault Millau praised the highly creative cuisine and culinary skill of this restaurant and gave it three chefs hats. The French chef then decided to close the restaurant and open a 'little bistro' with less ambitiuous food using regional produce such as Kvarner scampi, Istrian truffles and Adriatic seabream at affordable prices.

➕ 212 B2 ✉ Petilovrijenci 4 ☎ 020 321 168;
www.gilsdubrovnik.com 🕙 Daily 7pm–11pm

Lokanda Peskarija ££

Locals come here for good, fresh, simply cooked seafood, right next to the harbour. Choose from mussels, prawns, oysters, squid, grilled fish or seafood risotto, served with salad and dry white wine. At lunchtime make sure you arrive at Lokanda Peskarija early or be prepared to wait.

➕ 212 C2 ✉ Na Ponti ☎ 020 324 750
🕙 Daily 8am–midnight

Mea Culpa £

For a good-value lunch, you can't beat this popular pizzeria in the back streets of the Old Town. The pizzas are cooked in a wood-fired oven. Other choices include Italian classics such as lasagne and salads. There are a few tables inside, but most people eat outside on the cobbled street.

➕ 212 A2 ✉ Za Rokom 3 ☎ 020 323 430
🕙 Daily 8am–midnight

Orhan £££

This smart fish restaurant outside Pile Gate is one of Dubrovnik's best-kept secrets. Take the steps down to the waterfront beneath the Lovrijenac Fortress and you will find it among the upturned fishing boats, beside a peaceful cove which once served as the town's main harbour. On summer evenings, you can dine on a covered terrace right beside the sea. The house special is fresh fish, brought to your table on a tray to help you make your choice. If you don't want the fish, other options include steaks, schnitzel, risotto and pasta dishes.

➕ 212 off A2 ✉ Od Tabakarije 1
☎ 020 414 183 🕐 Daily 11am–midnight

Sesame ££

This tavern beyond Pile Gate is popular with students. The walls are lined with old theatre posters and programmes for the Dubrovnik Summer Festival dating back 50 years, as well as a grenade from the Croation War of Independence. The restaurant has separate lunch and dinner menus, both Mediterranean in flavour but with a handful of good pasta dishes and unusual salads such as smoked ham with figs or octopus with cheese. Vegetarians are well catered for too – try the vegetable sorbet, courgette carpaccio and pasta with truffles.

➕ 212 off A2 ✉ Ulica Dante Alighierija
☎ 020 412 910 🕐 Daily 8am–11pm

KORČULA

Adio Mare ££

A touristy but atmospheric place to eat in Korčula is this down-to-earth tavern near the cathedral, with stone walls and communal wooden tables and benches. The menu, which has hardly changed for 30 years, features Dalmatian classics like *brudet* (fish soup with polenta), *pržolica* (beef with cabbage) and *pasticada* (stewed veal with onions, tomatoes and prunes), along with steaks and kebabs that are barbecued on a charcoal fire in the

corner. Tip: No reservation is possible, so arrive early.

➕ 204 B2 ✉ Ulica Svetog Roka 2, Korčula town ☎ 020 711 253 🕐 Apr–Oct daily 6pm–midnight

Maslina £

This small family-run restaurant is set among olive groves on the road from Korčula to Lumbarda. House specials include macaroni and *pogača*, a pizza-like dish of crusty bread topped with tomatoes, onions, peppers, aubergines, courgettes, olive tapenade and melted cheese. You can also eat outside on the terrace in the summer (no sea view!).

➕ 199 F2 ✉ Lumbarajska Cesta ☎ 020 711 720 🕐 Summer daily 11am–midnight

Morski Konjic ££

This long terrace restaurant takes up virtually the whole of the eastern promenade, with tables on the sea walls looking across the water to the Pelješac peninsula. The wide-ranging menu includes meat and fish dishes such as plain grilled fish, mussels and octopus salad, washed down with the local Grk and Pošip wines.

➕ 204 B2 ✉ Šetalište Petra Kanavelića
☎ 020 711 878 🕐 Apr–Oct daily 8am–1am

PELJEŠAC

Kapetanova Kuća ££

People come from far and wide to sample the local oysters at Mali Ston which are famed for their aphrodisiac qualities. There are several good restaurants on the picturesque waterfront but 'the Captain's House' is the best, offering fresh, grilled oysters, oyster soup and beef in oyster sauce, as well as local mussels, lobster and fresh fish. Mali Ston has become a very popular honeymoon destination and the owners of Kapetanova Kuća also run a small boutique hotel called Hotel Ostrea (££).

➕ 205 D2 ✉ Mali Ston ☎ 020 754 555, www.ostrea.hr 🕐 Daily 9am–midnight

Where to ...
Shop

DUBROVNIK

The shops along Stradun are designed to appeal mainly to tourists to Dubrovnik, offering the typical articles you would expect in a holiday destination: T-shirts, souvenirs, postcards, books and CDs. For a wide range of foreign-language books about Croatia, visit the branch of **Algoritam** (Stradun 8). Most of the Old Town bookshops sell books and videos about Dubrovnik during the siege of 1991–92.

For more unusual boutiques you need to leave Stradun and explore the narrow streets to the south.

Od Puča is the main shopping street in the Old Town, with small off-beat shops specialising in costume jewellery, clothing, antiques and modern works of art. Several shops at the western end of **Od Puča** sell intricate gold and silver jewellery in filigree designs, a speciality of Dubrovnik since the days of the Ragusan republic.

If you're after a silk tie, a branch of **Croata** is at Pred Dvorom 2, next to the cathedral.

The chemist's in the cloisters of the **Franjevački Samostan** (Franciscan monastery, ▶ 153) sells herbal remedies dating back to 1317.

The morning market in **Poljana Gundulićeva**, at the eastern end of Od Puča, is a lively affair, with farmers selling cheese, fruit liqueurs and fresh produce.

For Dalmatian wines and spirits, visit **Vinoteka** (Stradun) or **Dubrovačka Kuća** (Ulica Svetog Dominika), not far from weit Ploče Gate.

Where to ...
Go Out

CAVTAT

There are all sorts of events held during **Cavtat Summer Festival** including performances by a *klapa* choir of a-cappella songs.

DUBROVNIK

During the **Dubrovnik Summer Festival** there are more than 80 performances of plays, operas and ballets on open-air stages in the Old Town as well as concerts of ancient music and dances performed in historical costume. The festival starts each year with a fireworks display on 10 July and finishes on 25 August. For information contact the festival office (tel: 020 326 100, www.dubrovnik-festival.hr) or visit the kiosks on Stradun and at Pile Gate.

During the summer, the Linđo folk ensemble perform on Monday and Friday evenings at Lazareti, the former quarantine hospital outside Ploče Gate. Jazz fans should head for **Troubadour**, a bar in Bunićeva Poljana, for live jazz at 10pm most nights in summer. Night owls party away in the EastWest Beach Club (▶ 154) on Banje beach or in the Latino Club Fuego.

KORČULA

The *moreška* sword dance (▶ 28) is performed Monday and Thursday evenings in summer next to Land Gate and at festivals, the biggest being on 29 July. For further information and tickets contact local travel agents.

Walks & Tours

1 ZAGREB OLD TOWN
Walk

DISTANCE 2.7km (1.6mi)
TIME 1–1.5 hours
START/FINISH Trg Bana Jelačića ✚ 211 F3

This short walk, beginning and ending in Zagreb's central square, explores the oldest and most attractive part of the capital – the maze of narrow streets and squares known as Gornji Grad (Upper Town). A funicular tramway takes you up the hill, avoiding a steep ascent on foot. Although it is possible to complete this walk in an hour, it is best to allow half a day to enjoy the various churches and museums along the way, go shopping in Dolac market and soak up the atmosphere of this historic district.

❶–❷
Start in **Trg Bana Jelačića** (▶ 48) next to the statue of the governor Josip Jelačić on horseback. With your back to the statue, look half-right and head for Kavana Dubrovnik, with outdoor tables on

Zagreb's funicular connects the upper and lower towns

the corner of Ulica Ljudevita Gaja (also known as **Gajeva**, ▶ 172). This is the entrance to a busy pedestrianised area of shops, cafés and ice-cream parlours which is particularly animated on summer evenings. Walk down Gajeva and turn right opposite the glass façade of the Hotel Dubrovnik into Ulica Mirka Bogovića (Bogovićeva), a busy promenade lined with open-air cafés and bars. The street ends in **Trg Petra Preradovića**, a large square with more cafés and a cinema.

❷–❸
Turn right here, passing the statue of Petar Preradović (1818–72), a soldier and romantic poet. Just beyond the statue is the meeting place of the town's Serbian minority, the Serbian Orthodox Church, that remained remarkably untouched during the conflict with Serbia in the 1990s.

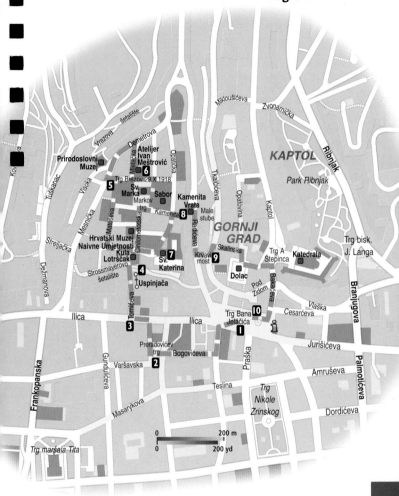

Emerging on Ilica, Zagreb's main shopping street, turn left and take he first right into **Ulica Tomića** (**Tomićeva**).

❸–❹

Now you have a choice. The easy option is to take the funicular (*uspinjača*) that runs every 10 minutes from 6:30am to 10pm. This delightful ride, the oldest form of public transport in Zagreb, first opened in 1893 as a steam-powered railway and was electrified

in 1943 – with a speed of 1.5m (5ft) per second and a journey time of under a minute. Alternatively, you can climb the flight of steps next to the tram to reach the Upper Town of Gradec.

❹–❺

Emerging from the funicular station, a leafy promenade, **Strossmayerovo Šetalište**, runs both left and right, following the route of the Old Town walls. Ignore this and keep straight ahead, passing to the right

Walks & Tours

of the Tower of **Lotrščak** with a glimpse of the coloured roof tiles of **St Mark's Church** (**Sv. Marka**) up ahead. Take the first left along Ulica Vranicanijeva and turn right along **Ulica Matoša** (**Matoševa**), passing the Hrvatski Povijesni Muzej (Croatian History Museum) on your left.

5–6

At the end of this street, turn left and immediately right onto **Ulica Mesnička** where you will see the **Prirodoslovni Muzej** (Natural History Museum), an eclectic collection housed in an old theatre, on your left. Follow this street until you reach a Classical-style archway leading to a school. Turn right here along Ulica Mletačka, passing the **Atelijer Ivan Meštrović** (► 54) on your left. Turn left at the end of the street to enter **Markov trg** (St Mark's Square).

6–7

This square is the symbolic heart of Croatia, lined with Baroque palaces and government buildings. On one side is the **Sabor** (Croatian parliament), on the other the presidential offices in the former Banski Dvor (Governor's Palace). It was this building that was hit by

As you walk through Zagreb, look out for details such as this sign on a wall in Kaptol

a Serbian rocket attack in October 1991 when President Tuđman was holding a cabinet meeting here – an event described in detail in the **City Museum** (► 56).

Cross to the far side of the square for the best views of St Mark's Church, then continue walking downhill in the direction of the Tower of Lotrčšak, passing the **Hrvatski Muzej Naivne Umjetnosti** (Naïve Art Museum, ► 56) and Greek Orthodox Church of St Cyril and St Methodius on your right. Returning to the crossroads just before the tower, turn left to see St Catherine's Church (**Sv. Katerina**). This is the town's Baroque masterpiece, with sculptures of the Virgin Mary and the four Apostles on the façade.

STREET NAMES

Most streets in Zagreb have at least two different names – the one seen on street signs and the one used by locals and on maps. Thus Ulica Gaja is also called Gajeva, Ulica Bogovića – Bogovićeva and Ulica Tomića – Tomićeva, Ulica Radića – Radićeva and Ulica Tkalčića –Tkalčićeva. To confuse matters further, the square which is officially known as Trg Petra Preradovića, near the start of this walk, is universally referred to by the locals as Cvjetni Trg (Flower Square) because of the flower market that is still held there.

7 – 8

Turn left next to the church to enter Jezuitski Trg where the former Jesuit monastery is now an art gallery hosting temporary exhibitions. At the crossroads, notice the old apothecary on the corner of Ulica Kamenita, in business since the mid-14th century. Turn right to walk through **Kamenita Vrata** (Stone Gate), one of the four original entrances to the walled town of Gradec. According to legend, after much of the Old Town was destroyed by fire in 1731, a painting of the Virgin Mary was discovered completely undamaged in the ashes. To celebrate this miracle, the gate was rebuilt and it now houses a shrine, full of flickering candles and devout pilgrims at prayer.

8 – 9

After passing through the gate, take the steps to the right next to the George and Dragon statue and turn right along Ulica Radića (Radićeva), a steep cobbled street lined with art galleries and souvenir shops. Turn left onto **Krvavi Most** (Bloody Bridge), the historic boundary between the townships of Kaptol and Gradec, whose name reflects the violent confrontations that used to take place between the two. Looking up, the spires of the cathedral are visible above the houses. Cross the bridge to reach **Ulica Tkalčića** (Tkalčićeva), one of the town's most attractive promenades with 19th-century houses that are now home to fashionable boutiques and trendy, youthful bars. The street lies on the dried-up channel of the former stream which once separated Kaptol from Gradec.

9 – 10

Turn left and then right onto Ulica Skalinska to arrive on the upper level of **Dolac market**, with clothes stalls in the street to your left and farmers selling fresh produce down

The richly decorated nave of St Catherine's Church in the Upper Town

below. Take the steps down to the main market square and continue in the same direction towards the **katedrala** (cathedral, ► 58). When you reach the street, Kaptol, with the cathedral directly ahead of you, turn right to return into **Trg Bana Jelačića**.

TAKING A BREAK

Mala Kavana, on the northern side of Trg Bana Jelačića close to the equestrian statue, is an old-style café serving good coffee and cakes. For drinks, just take your pick of the trendy bars along Ulica Tkalčića (Tkalčićeva). A good place for lunch is **Kerempuh** (► 63), on the upper level of Dolac market.

2 ZAGORJE
Tour

DISTANCE 148km (92mi), plus 10km (6mi) taking in the diversion to Trakošćan	
TIME 3.5 hours	
START/FINISH Marija Bistrica ✚ 206 C3	

This scenic drive is a round trip of the Zagorje (➤ 75), a rural region of cornfields, meadows, vineyards, pretty villages, hilltop churches and fairy-tale castles between Zagreb and the Slovenian border. Although you could easily spend several days exploring this region, it is possible to cover the main sights in a day trip from Zagreb, adding around two hours to the total time.

❶–❷

Start in the pilgrimage town of **Marija Bistrica** (➤ 76) and take the road to Donja Stubica. The road out of town is not well signposted, so it is easier to take the main road to Zagreb south of the church and turn right when you reach a junction on the edge of town. Stay on this gentle road as it winds through the peaceful Stubica valley beneath the northern slopes of **Mount Medvednica** (➤ 60) with its TV mast visible on the summit. The first village of any size is Gornja Stubica, known as the birthplace of a Peasant's Revolt in 1573 that is commemorated in the Muzej Seljačkih Buna (Museum of Peasant Uprisings). Shortly afterwards, you reach the lovely village of Donja Stubica, where a road next to the church square leads to the summit of Sljeme, providing a spectacular drive to Zagreb.

❷–❸

Continue on this road through the spa town of Stubičke Toplice. Where the road bends right, following signs to Zabok. After a further 2km (1.2mi), turn left at a roundabout towards Zabok. The road crosses the Zagreb-Krapina motorway, by-passes Zabok and continues for 20km (12.5mi) to **Kumrovec** (➤ 84), rising and then falling to the dramatic Sutla valley, right on the Slovenian border. Shortly before Kumrovec, you enter the Zelenjak Gorge, with the forested hills of Slovenia visible across the river. On your right, you pass the Lijepa Naša monument, a stone obelisk dedicated to local poet Antun Mihanović (1796–1861), the author of the Croatian national anthem (➤ 176).

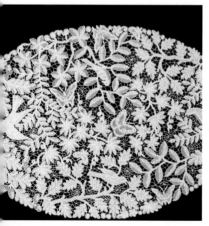

Lace-making is a regional speciality

3–4

Just after passing Kumrovec, you reach a fork in the road where you must keep right to Miljana – a left fork would take you to a Slovenian border post instead. Note the hilltop church on the horizon, high above the thickly wooded slopes. Now you are in the rural heart of the Zagorje, all farmsteads, barns and roadside shrines and cottages offering *seoski turizam* (agritourism, ▶ 18). The road climbs to the village of

Zagorska Sela, dominated by the Church of Sveta Katerina, before continuing to Miljana.

4–5

Turn right here towards Desinić or you will soon reach another border post. Shortly you will see the castle of **Veliki Tabor** (▶ 75) perched on a hill to your left. After exploring the castle, drive through the village of Desinić and take the left fork towards Pregrada.

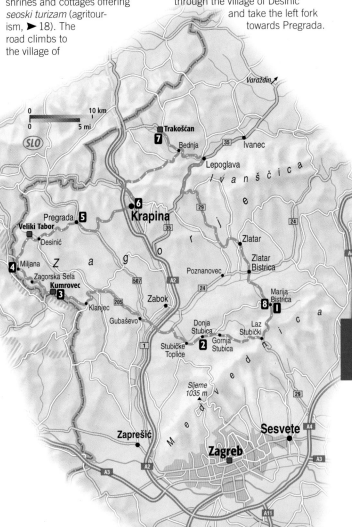

The path below the castle walls at Trakošćan

5–6

Arriving in Pregrada, turn right along the main street, following signs to Zagreb. After 5km (3mi), turn left next to the Dvorec Bežanec hotel and stay on this road as it climbs and descends through the vineyards, before dropping steeply to Krapina (► 77).

6–7

Turn left as you enter Krapina, passing the **Muzej Evolucije**

TAKING A BREAK
Grešna Gorica (Taborgradska 3, Desinić, tel: 049 343 001, open daily 10–10, ► 89).

Husnjakovo (Museum of Evolution) on your left. Continue on this road as it runs next to the railway line, then turn right, signposted to Varaždin, passing beneath the busy motorway high overhead. Stay on this minor country road to reach the village of Bednja, with its oversized church with a cream-coloured façade. A short diversion left at this point leads in 5km (3mi) to the castle at Trakošćan (► 75f).

7–8

To complete the main route, turn right towards Lepoglava, the site of a notorious prison where both Tito and Franjo Tuđman were incarcerated. The prison, the largest in Croatia, occupies the site of a former monastery, built by monks of the Order of St Paul who also established Croatia's first grammar school and university here. In Lepoglava, turn right and follow the railway line for the next 5km (3mi). Reaching a junction, turn left, passing through Zlatar and Zlatar Bistrica on the way back to Marija Bistrica.

3 ISTRIAN HILL TOWNS
Tour

DISTANCE 68km (42mi)
TIME 1.5 hours
START/FINISH Pazin ✛ 198 B4

Although they lie just a short distance inland from the busy coastal resorts, the hill towns of Istria offer a completely different experience. Even if you are staying by the sea in Poreč, Pula or Rovinj, it is worth renting a car for the day and heading inland to the vineyards, olive groves and oak woods. This short, easy circuit takes in two of the most dramatic hill towns, though it can easily be extended to include others (▶ 105) or taken as a leisurely half-day excursion from the coast.

❶–❷
Begin in **Pazin** which can be reached on the fast road connecting

Rijeka with Rovinj and Pula. This small industrial town with a population of around 10,000 may not have immediate appeal, but it is worth a flying visit. The highlight is the castle, first mentioned in 983AD as a gift of Emperor Otto II of Hungary to the bishop of Poreč. The castle, now an ethnographic museum (summer Tue–Sat 10–4, 18kn), overlooks a great gorge known as Pazin's Pit, where the River Pazinčica swells after rain, almost encircling the town.

The fortified walls of the hilltop town of Buzet

Walks & Tours

Although he never visited Pazin, the French novelist Jules Verne (1828–1905) was inspired by the pit and the little river that disappears underground – the hero of his novel, *Mathias Sandorf*, was imprisoned in the castle and escaped by swimming along the underground river to the sea.

Leave Pazin by taking the main road through the middle of town in the direction of Rijeka and the Učka Tunnel. After 2km (1.2mi), you will see a right turn leading to the motorway to Rijeka. Ignore this and keep straight ahead, crossing fertile countryside with the peaks of Učka, often covered in snow, rising in the distance. After 8km (5mi), you come to the village of Cerovjle. There are many ancient

villages and churches perched on hilltops in this region.

2 – 3

Turn left immediately before the level crossing on the old road to Buzet and left again at the next junction. The road now rises to Kovačići from where a panoramic view of central Istria opens out in front of you. Ahead and to the left is the Butoniga valley, with a lake in the middle and views across the plain to the hill town of Motovun in the distance; to the right is the Čičarija ridge, dividing Istria from Slovenia and the rest of Croatia.

Shortly afterwards, you reach the village of **Draguć**, little more than a single road of houses and a tall church perched on a cliff. In the 1970s and 1980s, Draguć was known as the 'Istrian Hollywood' as a number of films were shot here, but these days the village is largely deserted. The 12th-century Romanesque Chapel of St Elisium (Sv. Elisej) and the 14th-century St Rok's Church (Sv. Rok) are both renowned for their frescoes. The latter, painted by Master Anthony of Padova, features vivid images of biblical scenes including the Adoration of the Magi and the Annunciation. The churches are normally kept locked, but if you want to have a look inside, ask around in the village and you may find the keyholder who will let you in for a small donation.

3 – 4

The road continues as far as **Buzet**, the largest of the hill towns, on a bluff 151m (495ft) above the River Mirna and still partly enclosed by its medieval walls and gates. Buzet has more recently become Istria's self-styled 'town of truffles' and each autumn it attracts a large

One of the Slavonic alphabet stones along Glagolitic Alley, showing a letter in the Cyrillic alphabet

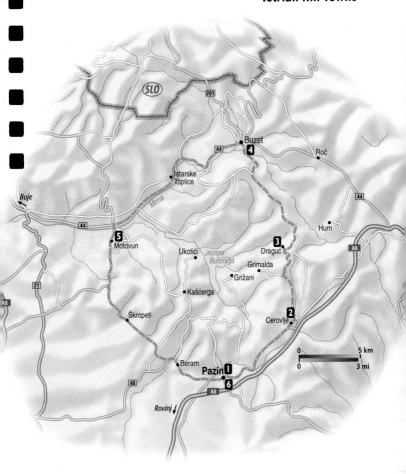

GLAGOLITIC ALLEY

A short diversion along the road from Buzet to Rijeka leads to **Roč**, the start of the so-called 'Glagolitic Alley'. This 7km (4mi) **sculpture trail** between Roč and Hum commemorates the Glagolitic script, a 41-letter **Slavonic alphabet** devised in the 9th century by the Greek brothers St Cyril and St Methodius who were instrumental in converting Croatia to Christianity. The script was widely used in liturgical texts in Croatia between the 11th and 19th centuries and the first known printing of a Glagolitic missal took place in Istria in 1483. There are 11 **sculptures** along the trail which recall **significant events** and important symbols in Istrian and Croatian history. Look out for the stone featuring the Glagolitic, Latin and Cyrillic alphabets – Glagolitic was a forerunner of Cyrillic which is named after St Cyril and is still used in Russia, Bulgaria and Serbia today. The trail ends in Hum, the self-proclaimed 'smallest town in the world', with just 23 inhabitants, an annual election for mayor and a copper town gate engraved in Glagolitic script.

Motovun sits majestically on a hilltop in the middle of the landscape

number of visitors who come here to taste and buy this expensive delicacy.

4–5

At Buzet, turn left to follow the main road along the **Mirna valley** towards Buje. Pass the spa town of **Istarske Toplice** where the waters have been known for their healing properties since Roman times. Stay on this road as it continues through the narrow valley with oak woods and tall crags to either side. When you reach a crossroads, turn left and take the bridge across the river towards **Motovun** (➤ 105), the best known and most spectacularly sited of the Istrian hill towns. After another 2km (1.2mi),

you can park at the foot of the hill or carry on up to another car park below the town gate where you have to pay.

5–6

Stay on this road and turn left at a junction to return to Pazin. Along the way you will pass the small village of **Beram**, noted for its 15th-century cycle of frescoes in the chapel of the Virgin Mary which is just outside the village. It features a macabre Dance of the Dead, depicting not only skeletons, but a rich gallery of human characters from medieval Istria. The message behind these frescoes is, of course, that all humans are equal at the hour of death.

4 DUBROVNIK OLD TOWN

Walk

DISTANCE 3km (2 mile)
TIME 1 hour
START/FINISH Vrata od Pile (Pile Gate) ⊞ 212 A2

One highlight in Dubrovnik is a walk around the town walls (P153), but it can be just as rewarding to stroll inside the ramparts, discovering hidden lanes and courtyards in the oldest parts of the town. Even when Stradun is thronging with people, it is usually possible to find a quiet corner just a few streets away.

This short walk explores the narrow lanes rising above Stradun to either side, so involves a fair degree of climbing. Most local buses stop outside Pile Gate, the starting point of the walk. However, if you arrive by boat from Cavtat at the old harbour, you will need to walk the length of Stradun to reach the start.

1 – 2

Begin just inside **Pile Gate** next to **Onofrio Fountain.** This large domed structure, with water spouting from sculpted masks, is a popular meeting place where buskers enter-tain the crowds. The fountain was completed in 1444 by the Neapolitan engineer Onofrio della Cava to supply fresh water to the town. It was badly damaged during the earthquake of 1667 and again during the siege of 1991–92, but has now been restored in part to its former glory. The nearby Church of **Sveti Spasa** (St Saviour) is used for summer evening concerts.

The Pile Gate entrance into the walled town

MEDIEVAL GRAFFITI

From Ulica Od Puča, near the start of the walk, a few yards along Ulica Zlatarica is one of Dubrovnik's hidden gems. Look carefully and you will see some graffiti, dated 1597, etched into the outside wall of St Rok's Church. Translated from the Latin, it serves as a warning to children playing ball in the street: 'I'm warning you, players .. .peace be with you, but remember that you will die'.

Walks & Tours

Take a stroll along the Old Town walls

Walk straight ahead along **Stradun**, whose limestone paving has been polished to a sheen by the many feet passing this way over the centuries. Almost immediately, look for an archway to your right and pass beneath it into **Ulica Gariste**. At the next crossroads, turn left into **Ulica Od Puča**, the main shopping street of the Old Town. There are several good jewellery shops here selling the distinctive local gold and filigree silverwork, as well as art galleries, haberdashers and wine shops.

2–3

Turn right at **Ulica Široka**, passing **Dom Marina Držića**, the former home of the playwright Marin Držić (1508–67) on your left. Držić was known for his bawdy comedies, performed in the fashionable Renaissance salons of Dubrovnik, Venice and Zagreb. The house is now a museum, with audiovisual displays giving an insight into 16th-century society. Continue straight ahead and climb the steps next to the Domino steak house, then turn right along Ulica Od Rupa. A short distance along on your left is the **Etnografski Muzej Rupe**, (April–Oct daily 9–6, Nov–March Mon–Fri 9–2, 25kn), an ethnographic museum in the former town granary, with deep storage pits carved out of the rock. The terrace in front of the museum has fine views over Dubrovnik and Mount Srđ in the northeast, to which the town owes its strategically favourable position and pleasant climate.

3–4

Turn left next to the museum to ascend the narrow flight of steps **Ulica Od Šorte**. As you climb, notice the protruding stone struts on the fronts of the houses, with pierced holes through which washing lines would be suspended for drying laundry or woollen yarn (Dubrovnik was known for its textiles in medieval times). At the top of the street, turn left to walk next to the former **Benedictine convent of St Mary**. After being ransacked and dissolved by Napoleonic troops during the French occupation (1805–15), the convent became a barracks and later a military hospital and is now flats. The entrance to the main courtyard features a relief of the Annunciation beneath the coats of arms of Dubrovnik and of noble families.

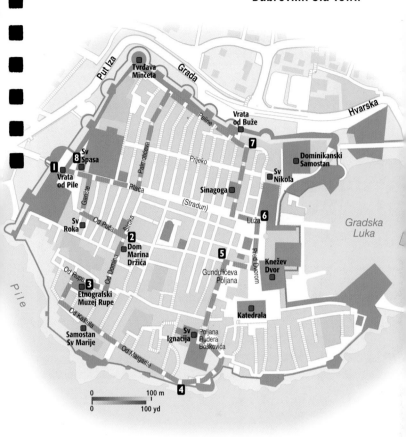

Stay on this cobbled path through one of the oldest and highest districts of the town until you come to some peaceful garden allotments beneath the town walls. The path now drops steeply next to the walls and a gap in the wall to your right (incongruously signposted 'Cold Drinks' in English) leads to a bar in a stunning location. It is certainly worth spending an hour here in summer, sitting beneath a palm tree on the side of the cliffs and gazing at the island of Lokrum across the sea.

4–5

Keep next to the walls as they bend left beneath the bastion of Sveta Margarita. Looking to your left, you can see the **Jesuit Church** (Sv. Ignacija) dominating the market square of **Poljana Ruđera Boškovića**. Completed in 1725, this is the largest church in Dubrovnik and its interior in particular is based on the 'mother church' of the Jesuit order, Il Gesu in Rome – a riot of Baroque excess with marble altars and mosaic tiles. Cross the square and walk down the monumental Jesuit Steps, built in 1738 to provide a suitably grand approach to the church and based on the Spanish Steps in Rome.

The steps end in **Gundulićeva Poljana** which is busy each morning

The inner courtyard of the Rectors' Palace

when farmers sell fresh fruit, vegetables and herbs, as well as bottles of lavender oil and strings of dried peppers and figs. At the heart of the square is a statue of Ivan Gundulić (1589–1638), Dubrovnik's greatest poet and a key figure in Croatian literature. The pedestal is decorated with scenes from his poem, *Osman*, describing a victory by the Polish army over the Ottoman Turks.

5–6

Turn right next at the statue to emerge on Pred Dvorom in front of the Rector's Palace (**Knežev Dvor**) with the cathedral to your right, then turn left to reach **Luža**, the broad square which marks the eastern end of Stradun. Above you is the 15th-century clock tower, heavily rebuilt, with a clock with numerals added in the early 20th century. Peer up to the top of the belfry and you may just be able to make out Maro and Baro, reconstructions of the original bronze figures who strike the hours with their hammers. Beneath the tower is a small fountain designed by Onofrio della Cava.

In the middle of the square is another Dubrovnik landmark, the statue of an armoured knight at the foot of Orlando Column. This remarkably gentle-looking figure is based on the cult of Orlando, the local name for the hero of the French epic poem *Chanson de Roland*. The original Roland was killed in battle in the Pyrenees, but the legend has been reinvented and has him ambushed by Saracens

The Stradun that runs east to west through the town

while defending Dubrovnik during the Crusades. During the time of the Ragusan Republic, when Dubrovnik was an independent city-state, new laws were proclaimed at the Orlando Column and the statue's right arm was used as a unit of measurement (51.2cm/20 inches).

6 – 7

Turn left along **Stradun** and take the second right onto **Ulica Žudioska**. This was the main street of the 16th-century Jewish ghetto, whose gates were locked each night to keep the Jewish population in. A short way up on the left is the synagogue that still serves a small Jewish community today and also contains an interesting museum (open summer daily 10–8, winter Mon–Fri 10–3, 25kn).

At the top of the first flight of steps, cross over **Prijeko**, the main thoroughfare of the upper town, running parallel to Stradun. Glance to your right to see the little Church of **St Nicholas** (**Sv. Nikola**) at the end of the street, with the Dominican monastery behind it. Continue climbing to the top of **Ulica Žudioska** to reach Peline.

7 – 8

Now you are in the highest part of town. Turn left along **Peline**, passing **Buža Gate** (Vrata od Buža), one of five town gates. Take the right fork and continue along Peline as it clings to the inside of the ramparts on its way to Minčeta Tower (**Tvrđava Minčeta**), a two-storey, circular fortress. The steep, narrow lanes to your left provide a series of wonderful vistas over the Old Town and back down to Stradun through a jumble of washing lines, little balconies, winding flights of steps and pot plants. Turn left along Palmotićeva or any of the other streets to return to Stradun.

TAKING A BREAK

There are numerous bars and cafés in the Old Town. For a drink with a view on a sunny day, you cannot beat Buža, reached through a gap in the town walls. A good spot for people-watching is Gradskavana's terrace, an old-style café between the clock tower and the Rector's Palace at Pred Dvorom 3. The restaurants along Prijeko are geared up for the tourist trade and mainly serve bland, over-priced food.

5 LOKRUM
Walk

DISTANCE 4km (2.5mi) plus boat trip
TIME 2–3 hours
START/FINISH Old Harbour, Dubrovnik ➕ 205 E1

The wooded island of Lokrum is Dubrovnik's summer garden where people go to escape the town, to walk, swim and sunbathe, to breathe fresh air and have a romantic break. A day out on Lokrum makes a relaxing change from sightseeing in Dubrovnik – take a boat to the island and you can then walk around the island in under two hours, but it is best to allow half a day, or bring your towel and swimming things and make a complete day of it.

Step ashore at the harbour and climb the ramp next to the jetty. On your right is the old forest ranger's house, destroyed by Serbian shells in 1991 and now left abandoned as a memorial. From here,

a well-signed network of walks leads across the island.

Take the footpath behind the house and stay on this shady lane as it clings to the northern shore, with occasional tracks through the trees leading to rocky beaches and bathing platforms. When the path forks, keep right above the shore, dropping down to reach the **Cross of Triton** (Tritonov Kriz) which commemorates the victims of a shipwreck in 1859.

Bear left above a small jetty and climb into the woods, leaving the shore behind. You soon reach **Lazaret**, the old isolation hospital, enclosed by high walls designed to prevent infections from spreading. Take the path to the right around

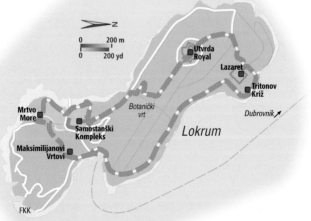

Boats make the scenic crossing from Dubrovnik to Lokrum regularly

Lazaret and continue climbing until you come to the highest point of the island, crowned by a ruined French fortress, **Fort Royal** (Utvrda Royal), dating from 1806. You can walk inside the star-shaped fort and climb the spiral staircase to the roof for 360-degree views of Dubrovnik, the whole of Lokrum and the sea as far south as Cavtat (▶ 163).

Leaving Fort Royal, take the path through the trees directly opposite where you entered and drop down towards the middle of the island along Rajski Put (Celestial Way), a processional route lined with tall cypress trees. Reaching a junction, turn right through the pine woods

THE LOKRUM CURSE

Do not visit Lokrum if you are superstitious. Ever since the 19th century, there has been persistent talk of 'the curse of Lokrum', perhaps placed by Benedictine monks in revenge for the destruction of their monastery. One owner, Archduke Maximilian, became emperor of Mexico but was killed by his subjects in 1867; the island later passed to his nephew, Crown Prince Rudolf, who committed suicide in 1889. Today the island is uninhabited and there are few people who would be willing to spend the night there.

BOAT TRIP

Boats depart regularly in summer from the Old Harbour in Dubrovnik; check the time of the last boat back (it is usually 6pm). The crossing takes 15 minutes; the price (60kn) for the trip includes the entrance fee to Lokrum.

and go down the steps beside a large reservoir, passing around the edge of a botanical garden. Turn left at the corner to walk through a beautiful wild olive grove with glimpses of the sea to your right. The **botanical gardens** (Botaniäki Vrt) are on your left, with numerous varieties of cactus and palm trees and with peacocks strutting around.

Follow the path around to the right to reach the former

View across Lokrum and the Adriatic from the French fort

Benedictine monastery (Samostanski Kompleks). Although much of the building is off limits, you can wander around the ruined cloisters which lead to an ornamental garden with a belvedere looking out to sea. Beyond the monastery, a path heads down to a swimming and sunbathing area. Instead,

take the path signposted no. 4 to **Mrtvo More** (Dead Sea). Passing a children's playground, you reach this salt-water lake, connected to the sea by an underground channel. The water is shallow, so safe for children and non-swimmers.

Turn left onto path no. 5 to return to the monastery on a woodland path, arriving in the landscaped **Maximilian Gardens** (Maksimilijanovi Vrtovi), from where it is a short stroll back to the harbour. Alternatively, for a longer walk, a series of footpaths leads around the wilder southern shore of the island, dropping down to Lokrum's popular nudist beach, with its concrete bathing platforms and dreamy views across the water to Cavtat.

TAKING A BREAK

There is a **restaurant** inside the monastery **cloisters** which is open in high summer. At other times, a **small bar** near the **harbour** (open summer daily 9–6) sells sandwiches and cold drinks. A pleasant alternative is to buy food for a picnic in Dubrovnik and take it across to the island.

Insider Tip

Practicalities

Practicalities

WHAT YOU NEED

- ● Required
- ○ Suggested
- ▲ Not required

	UK	USA	Canada	Australia	Ireland	Netherlands
Passport/National Identity Card	●	●	●	●	●	●
Visa (regulations can change – check before booking)	▲	▲	▲	▲	▲	▲
Onward or Return Ticket	○	○	○	○	○	○
Health Inoculations (tetanus and polio)	▲	▲	▲	▲	▲	▲
Health Documentation (▶ 194, Health)	▲	▲	▲	▲	▲	▲
Travel Insurance	○	○	○	○	○	○
Driving Licence (national) for car hire	●	●	●	●	●	●
Car Insurance Certificate	●	●	●	●	●	●
Car Registration Document	●	●	●	●	●	●

WHEN TO GO

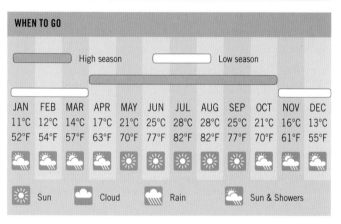

High season   Low season

JAN	FEB	MAR	APR	MAY	JUN	JUL	AUG	SEP	OCT	NOV	DEC
11°C	12°C	14°C	17°C	21°C	25°C	28°C	28°C	25°C	21°C	16°C	13°C
52°F	54°F	57°F	63°F	70°F	77°F	82°F	82°F	77°F	70°F	61°F	55°F

☀ Sun   ☁ Cloud   🌧 Rain   ⛅ Sun & Showers

The temperatures above are the **average daily maximum** for each month on the Adriatic islands and coast. Inland temperatures are considerably lower, often dropping below freezing in Zagreb and highland areas in winter. Snow is common in the mountains. During the summer, the sea temperature can be as high as 28°C. The best months to visit are May, June, September and October, when there is less traffic and fewer tourists, but the sea is still pleasantly warm. Late spring and early autumn are also good times for sailing and active holidays. The busiest months on the coast are July and August. Many hotels close down altogether between November and March.

GETTING ADVANCE INFORMATION

Websites
- ■ Croatian National Tourist Board: www.croatia.hr
- ■ Croatia web portal: www.hr

- ■ Ministry of Foreign Affairs (for visa information): www.mvpei.hr
- ■ Jadrolinija (ferry routes and timetables): www.jadrolinija.hr

Practicalities

GETTING THERE

By air There are **international airports** at Zagreb, Split, Dubrovnik, Pula, Rijeka and Zadar. Croatia Airlines (www.croatiaairlines.hr), has regular flights to Zagreb from major European cities, with additional flights to the coastal airports in summer. Links to North American cities are available through the Star Alliance network. Other airlines flying to Croatia include British Airways, Austrian Airlines and Lufthansa. **Budget airlines** flying to Croatia from the UK include easyJet (www.easyjet.com) to Split, Flybe (www.flybe.com) to Dubrovnik and Split, Ryanair (www.ryanair.com) to Pula and Zadar and Wizzair (www.wizzair.com) to Zagreb. There are also numerous **charter flights** from British and European cities in summer. Most seats on charter flights are allocated to tour operators, but flight-only deals are sometimes available online.

By sea Jadrolinija (www.jadrolinija.hr) operates **car and passenger ferries** between Italy and Croatia. The main routes are Ancona to Split, Ancona to Zadar and Bari to Dubrovnik, as well as the Adriatic coastal route linking Dubrovnik with Korčula, Stari Grad, Split and Rijeka. Foot passengers can generally buy tickets at the quayside, but car passengers should book in advance. Ferries from Italy to Croatia are also operated by SEM Marina (www.splittours.hr) and SNAV (www.snav.it). In summer, Venezia Lines (www.venezialines.com) and Triestelines (http://www.triestelines.it) operate high-speed links from Venice, Rimini and Ravenna to the Istrian coast.

By land Croatia shares **land borders** with Slovenia, Hungary, Bosnia-Hercegovina, Serbia and Montenegro. There are **bus and rail links** from Zagreb to most major European cities.

TIME

Croatia is on Central European Time, one hour ahead of Greenwich Mean Time. Summer time (GMT+2) operates from the last Sunday in March to the last Sunday in October.

CURRENCY AND FOREIGN EXCHANGE

Currency Croatia's currency is the **kuna** (which means 'marten'). The International Currency Code 'HRK' is only found when converting money, otherwise the abbreviation 'Kn' is used. The kuna is divided into 100 lipa. Coins are issued in denominations of 1, 2, 5, 10, 20 and 50 lipa, 1kn, 2kn and 5kn. Notes are issued in denominations of 5, 10, 20, 50, 100, 200, 500 and 1,000kn. The **euro (€)** is widely accepted at hotels.

Exchange As the exchange rate is more favourable in the country itself, it is recommended converting money on arrival. Apart from banks, there are lots of bureaux de change (*mjenjačnica*) that are generally open until late in the evening in the main tourist resorts. The exchange rate in hotels is often worse and a commission may be payable too. You can withdraw cash from ATM (cashpoint) machines in all towns and cities using your credit or debit card with your PIN. Your own bank will usually make a charge for this service.

Credit cards Major credit cards are widely accepted, though it is always advisable to have some cash with you especially in areas off the beaten tourist track.

CROATIAN NATIONAL TOURIST OFFICES

In the UK
2 The Lanchesters
162–164 Fulham Palace Road,
London W6 9ER
☎ 020 85 63 79 79

In the US
350 Fifth Avenue,
Suite 4003
New York, NY 10118
☎ 21 22 79 86 72

In France
Avenue Victor Hugo 48
75116 Paris
☎ 01 45 00 99 55

Practicalities

NATIONAL HOLIDAYS

1 Jan	New Year's Day
6 Jan	Epiphany
Mar/Apr	Easter Monday
1 May	Labour Day
May/Jun	Corpus Christi
22 Jun	Anti-Fascist Resistance Day
25 Jun	Croatian National Day
5 Aug	Victory Day
15 Aug	Feast of the Assumption
8 Oct	Independence Day
1 Nov	All Saints' Day
25–26 Dec	Christmas

ELECTRICITY

The power supply is 220 volts AC. Sockets take two-pinned round continental plugs.

Visitors from the UK will need an adaptor and visitors from the USA will need a transformer for 100–120 volt devices.

OPENING HOURS

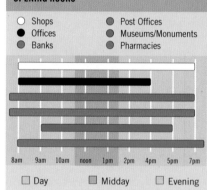

○ Shops
● Offices
● Banks
● Post Offices
● Museums/Monuments
● Pharmacies

8am 9am 10am noon 1pm 2pm 4pm 5pm 7pm

☐ Day   ☐ Midday   ☐ Evening

Shops Most are closed Sat afternoon and all day Sun. Shopping centres in Zagreb and in coastal resorts may stay open longer and on Sun.
Banks Generally open Mon–Fri 7–7, Sat 7–1.
Museums Opening hours vary widely. Many are closed on Mon and weekend afternoons. Main **post offices** are open Mon–Fri 7–7, Sat 7–1. Post offices in larger towns and cities stay open till 10pm.

TIPS/GRATUITIES

Tipping is not expected for all services and rates are generally lower than elsewhere.

Restaurants	10 ct
Taxis	10 ct
Tour guides	10–20kn
Chambermaids	10kn / night
Porters / Toilet attendants	No

SMOKING

In Croatia smoking is forbidden by law in public facilities. In some places, there are exceptions for small cafés and restaurants (up to 50m²) or there is a separate room for smokers.

TIME DIFFERENCES

Zagreb
12 noon

←
London (GMT)
11am

←
New York (EST)
6am

Germany (CET)
12 noon

→
Sydney (AEST)
9pm

Practicalities

STAYING IN TOUCH

Post: Stamps can be bought at post offices and news kiosks. Postboxes are yellow and marked HP. Letters to EU countries generally arrive within 5 to 10 days and to the US within two weeks. For urgent mail, use internet cafés in the main towns and resorts. In Croatia, a postcard to a European country costs 3.10kn, a letter 7.10kn.

Telephones: There are public telephones in all main towns. Phonecards (*telefonska kartica*) can be bought from post offices, news kiosks and shops with the HT (Hrvatski Telekom) logo. The international dialling code for Croatia is 385.

International dialling codes:
Dial 00 followed by

UK:	44
USA /Canada:	1
Irish Republic:	353
Australia:	61
Germany:	49

Mobile providers and services: Mobile phone coverage is almost universal; the main network operators are T-Com and VIP. Make sure your phone is switched to international roaming before you go. The international dialling code for Croatia is 385. A prepaid card bought in each place you stay may be cheaper. Such cards are called *bon za mobitel* in Croatian. A cell or mobile phone is a *mobilni telefon* or, more colloquially, *mobiltel*. Mobile numbers always begin with 09.

WiFi and Internet: There are public Internet cafés in all larger towns and tourist resorts. Many hotels have computer terminals or WiFi.

PERSONAL SAFETY

- Do not leave valuables on the beach or at the poolside.
- Always lock valuables in hotel safes or deposit boxes.
- Never leave anything inside your car. If you have to, lock it out of sight in the boot.
- Beware of pick-pockets in crowded markets and on buses and trams in Split, Dubrovnik and Zagreb.
- Avoid discussions of the recent war, especially in ethnic Serb areas close to the Bosnian and Serbian borders.
- Stick to marked footpaths in remote border areas and pay close attention to landmine warning signs.

Emergency calls:
☎ 112

	EMERGENCY CALLS	112
	POLICE	192
	FIRE	193
	AMBULANCE	194

Practicalities

HEALTH

 Insurance Citizens of EU countries receive free emergency medical treatment on production of their passport under a reciprocal health care agreement. This covers essential hospital stays, but excludes some expenses such as the cost of prescribed medicines. Private medical insurance is still advised and is essential for all other visitors.

 Dental services Dental treatment has to be paid for by all visitors, but is usually covered by private medical insurance.

 Sun The sun is intense on the Adriatic coast in summer and you can burn very quickly. Cover up with a high-factor sunscreen, wear a hat and drink plenty of water. Children are especially vulnerable and need to be protected, especially near the sea.

 Drugs Prescription and non-prescription drugs and medicines are available from pharmacies *(ljekarna)*. Outside normal hours, a notice on pharmacy doors gives the address of the nearest duty chemist. Take adequate supplies of any drugs you need regularly as they may not be available. Other items to consider include insect repellent, anti-diarrhoea pills and sea-sickness tablets if you are going to be using the ferries.

 Safe water Tap water is safe to drink. Bottled mineral water is widely available.

CONCESSIONS

Children/Students Children under 12 pay half-price on most buses, trains and ferries, while children under three go free. An international student identity card (ISIC) gives discounts at museums and on public transport.
Senior citizens Travellers over 60 may be entitled to discounted admission at museums and reduced fares on public transport.

TRAVELLING WITH A DISABILITY

Croatia has made great strides in providing facilities for travellers with disabilities, following a war in which many Croatians were disabled, but many older buildings are still inaccessible and cobbled streets in Dubrovnik and Zagreb are a particular problem for wheelchairs. Most modern hotels are suitable for disabled visitors. Enquire before booking.

CHILDREN

Hotels and restaurants are generally very child-friendly, many hotels and campsites have playgrounds and children's pools. Special attractions for kids are marked out with the logo shown above.

TOILETS

Toilets can be found at bus and train stations. They usually make a small charge.

CUSTOMS

Souvenirs from rare and endangered species may be illegal or require a special permit. Before buying, check your home country's customs regulations.

EMBASSIES AND CONSULATES (ZAGREB)

 UK
☎ 01 600 91 00

 USA
☎ 01 661 22 00

 Ireland
☎ 01 631 00 25

 Australia
☎ 01 489 12 00

 New Zealand
☎ 01 461 20 60

LANGUAGE

The official language of Croatia is Croatian (**hrvatski**). Until 1991, this was known as Serbo-Croat, but it is now recognised as a separate language. Unlike Serbian, which uses the Cyrillic script, Croatian uses the Latin alphabet, though otherwise many words are identical. Croatian is entirely phonetic which means that every word is pronounced exactly as it is written. Additional letters used in Croatian are č (pronounced 'ch'), ć (almost the same), š (pronounced 'h'), ž (pronounced like a 'j') and đ (pronouned 'dj'). The letter 'c' is pronounced 'ts' and 'j' is pronounced 'y'.

GENERAL

hi **bog**
hello/good day **dobar dan**
good morning **dobro jutro**
good evening **dobar večer**
goodbye **doviđenja**
how are you? **kako ste**
please **molim**
thank you **hvala**
excuse me **oprostite**
yes / no **da / ne**
here you are **izvolite**
cheers! **živjeli!**
large / small **veliko / malo**
cheap / expensive **jeftin / skupo**
Croatia **hrvatska**
America / England **amerika / engleska**
I don't understand **ne razumijem**
do you speak English? **govorite li engleski?**
open **otvoreno**
closed **zatvoreno**
excuse me **izvinite**
tourist office **turistički ured**
embassy **veleposlanstvo**
consulate **konzulami ured**
cathedral **katedrala**
church **crkva**
garden **vrt**
library **knijižnica**
doctor **liječnik/doktor**
dentist **zubar**
police **policija**
hospital **bolnica**
entrance / exit **ulaz / izlaz**

TIME

hour **sat**
minute **minuta**
week **tjedan**
day **dan**
today **danas**
tomorrow **sutra**
yesterday **jučer**

TRANSPORT

bus **autobus**
tram **tramvaj**
train **vlak**
bus station **autobusni kolodvor**
train station **zeljernički kolodvor**
airport **zračna luka**
port **luka**
ferry **trajekt**
ticket **karta**
timetable **vozni red**
arrival / departure **dolazak / odlazak**
taxi **taksi**
petrol **benzin**

SHOPPING

bakery **pekara**
bookshop **knijžara**
butchers **mesnica**
cake shop **slastičarna**
pharmacy **ljekarna**
market **tržnica**
travel agent **putnička agencija**

NUMBERS

0 nula	10 deset	20 dvadeset	101 sto i jedan
1 jedan	11 jedanaest	21 dvadeset jedan	200 dvjesto
2 dva	12 dvanaest	30 trideset	300 tristo
3 tri	13 trinaest	40 četrdeset	400 četristo
4 četiri	14 četrnaest	50 pedeset	500 petsto
5 pet	15 petnaest	60 šezdeset	600 šeststo
6 šest	16 šestnaest	70 sedamdeset	700 sedamsto
7 sedam	17 sedamnaest	80 osamdeset	800 osamsto
8 osam	18 osamnaest	90 devedeset	900 devetsto
9 devet	19 devetnaest	100 sto	1000 tisuću

Useful Words and Phrases

MONEY

bank banka
exchange **razmjena**
exchange **rate ečaj**
cashier **blagajnik**
money **novac**
cash **gotovina**
banknote **novčanice**
coin **kovani novac**
credit **card kreditna karta**
travellers' **cheque travel čekove**
post **office pošta**
stamp **poštanske marka**
postcard **razglednica**
telephone **card telekarta**

ACCOMMODATION

hotel **hotel**
room **soba**
single room **jednokrevetna soba**
double room **dvokrevetna soba**
apartment **apartman**

bath **kupaona**
shower **tuš**
toilet **zahod**
balcony **balkon**
telephone **telefon**
television **televizor**
breakfast **doručak**
half-board **polupansion**
key **ključ**
reservation **rezervacija**
campsite **autokamp**

RESTAURANT

restaurant **restauracija**
inn **konoba**
café **kavana**
cake **shop slastičarnica**
breakfast **doručak**
lunch **ručak**
dinner **večeru**
menu **jelovnik**
wine list **vinska karta**
the bill **račun**

MENU READER

barbun red mullet
bijelo vino
   white wine
blitva Swiss chard
breskva peach
brudet fish stew
čaj tea
čaj sa limunom
   tea with lemon
čevapčići
   spicy meatballs
crni rižot
   black risotto
crno vino red wine
češnjak garlic
cipal rey mullet
dagnje mussels
divlja svinija
   wild boar
džem jam
fiš paprikaš
   spicy fish stew
gazirana mineralna
   voda sparkling
   mineral water
govedina beef
grah beans
grčka cheese

grgeč perch
gulaš goulash
jabuka apple
jaje (jaja)
   egg (eggs)
janjetina lamb
jastog lobster
juha soup
kajmak
   clotted sour cream
kava coffee
krastavac cucumber
kruh bread
krumpir potatoes
kruške pears
kulen spicy salami
kupus cabbage
lignje squid
limun emon
losos salmon
   trout
lozovača brandy
luben bass
luk onion
marelica apricot
maslinovo ulje
   olive oil
meso meat

mješana salata
   mixed salad
musaka moussaka
naranča orange
negazarina
   mineralna voda
   still mineral water
njoki gnocchi
ocat vinegar
oštrige oysters
ovčetina mutton
palačinke pancakes
papar pepper
paprike
   green peppers
paški sir sheep's
   cheese
pašticada beef with
   dumplings
pastrva trout
piletina chicken
pomfrit chips
pršut dry-cured ham
ragu thick soup
rajčica tomato
rak crab
rakija spirit
ramsteak rump steak

riba fish
riža rice
roze vino rosé wine
sardina sardines
sarma stuffed
   cabbage or vine
   leaves
sir cheese
škampi crayfish
sladoled
   ice-cream
slan salt
špinat spinach
šunka ham
svinjetina pork
tartufi truffles
teletina veal
travarica
   spirit flavoured
   with herbs
tuna tuna
ulje oil
voće fruits
voda water
zelena lettuce
zelena salata
   green salad
zubatac bream

Road Atlas

For chapters: See inside front cover

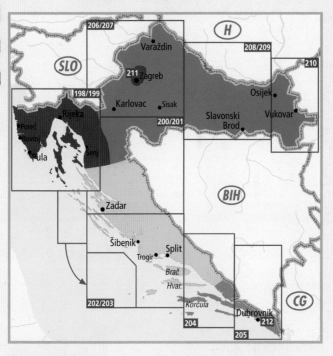

Key to Road Atlas

Motorway	![airport] International airport
Dual carriageway	Regional airport
Trunk road	Harbour, mooring
Main road	Border crossing
Secondary road	E 70 European Route number
Road under construction/development	★ Point of interest
Road closed for motor vehicles	Archaeological site
Tunnel	Monastery / Church
Railroad	Castle, fortress / Ruin
Ferry	Monument
International-, province boundary	Radio or TV tower / Lighthouse
National park, National preserve	Windmill
Restricted area	(Swimming) beach
	Waterfall / Cave, grotto
★ TOP 10	Mountain peak / Pass
26 Don't Miss	Campground
22 At Your Leisure	Spa
	Lookout point

1 : 710 000

0   25   50 km

0   15   30 mi

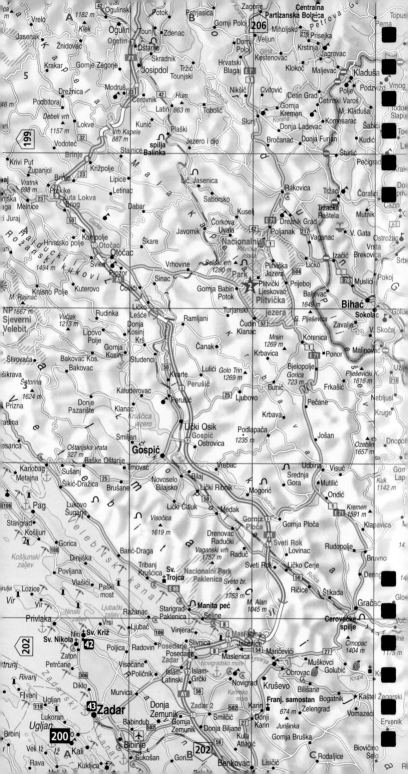

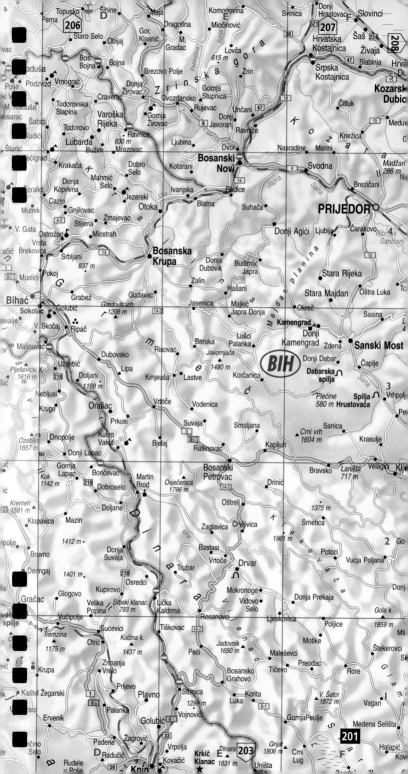

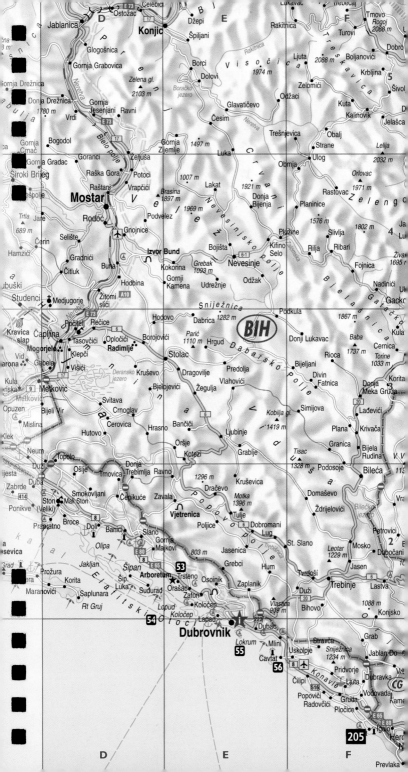

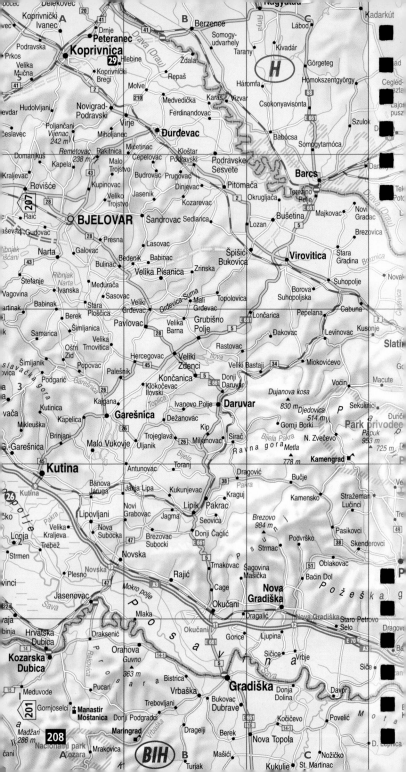

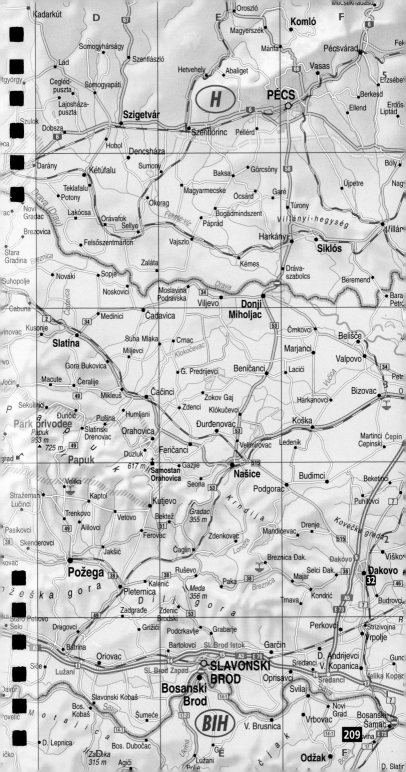

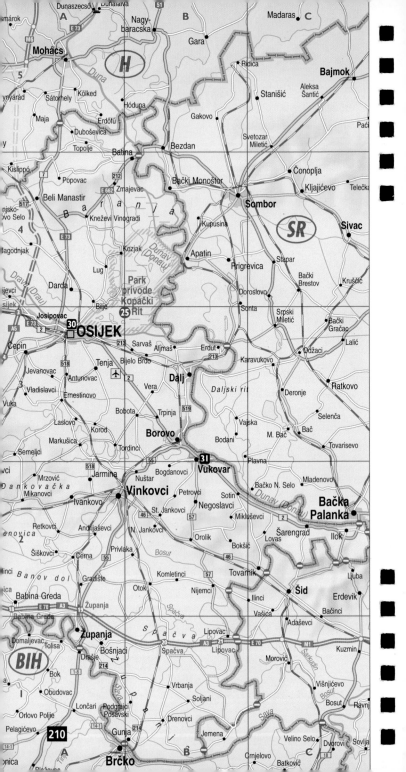

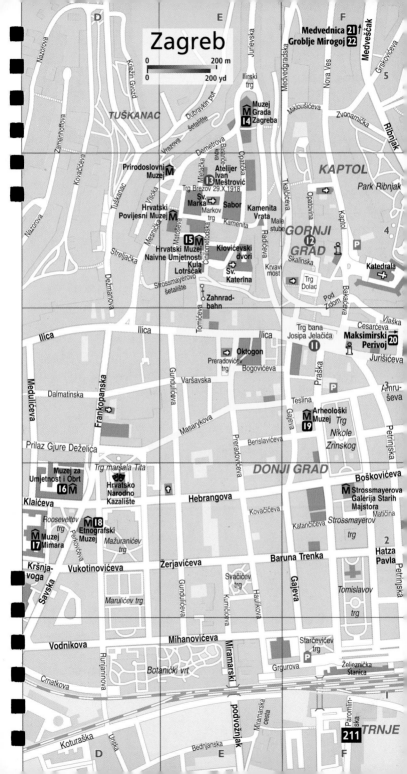

Zagreb

0 — 200 m
0 — 200 yd

Medvednica 21 ↑ *Medveščak*
Groblje Mirogoj 22

TUŠKANAC

Muzej Grada Zagreba M14

Prirodoslovni Muzej M

KAPTOL

Park Ribnjak

Atelijer Ivan Meštrović 13

Hrvatski Povijesni Muzej M

Sv. Marka

Sabor

Kamenita Vrata

GORNJI GRAD 12

Hrvatski Muzej Naivne Umjetnosti 15

Kloviićevski dvori

Male stube

Katedrala

Kula Lotrščak

Sv. Katerina

Trg Dolac

Krvavi most

Pod Zidom

Strossmayerovo šetalište

Zahnrad-bahn

Ilica

Trg bana Josipa Jelačića 11

Cesarčeva

Vlaška

Maksimirski Perivoj 20

Jurišićeva

Oktogon

Preradovićev trg

Bogovićeva

Praška

Arheološki Muzej M19

Teslina

Trg Nikole Zrinskog

DONJI GRAD

Berislavićeva

Boškovićeva

Muzej za Umjetnost i Obrt M16

Hrvatsko Narodno Kazalište

Hebrangova

Kovačićeva

Strossmayerova Galerija Starih Majstora M

Matičina

Strossmayerov trg

Katančićeva

Roosveltov trg

Muzej Mimara M17

Etnografski Muzej M18

Mažuranićev trg

Žerjavićeva

Baruna Trenka

Hatza Pavla

Klaićeva

Vukotinovićeva

Svačićev trg

Gajeva

Tomislavov trg

Kršnja-voga

Savska

Marulićev trg

Mihanovićeva

Starčevićev trg

Vodnikova

Botanički vrt

Grgurova

Željeznička Stanica

Cmatkova

Koturaška

Bednjanska

Paromlin-ska

211 *TRNJE*

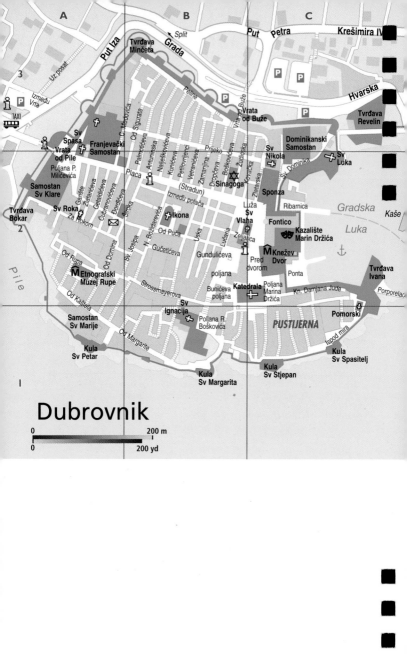

Dubrovnik

0		200 m
0		200 yd

Street Index

Zagreb

Amruševa	F3
Bakaćeva	F3/4
Baruna Trenka	E/F2
Basaričekova	E4/5
Bednjanska	E1
Berislavićeva	E/F3
Boškovićeva	F2
Bogovićeva	E3
Cesarćeva	F3
Ćinilometodska	E4
Crnatkova	D1
Dalmatinska	D3
Dežmanova	D3/4
Demetrova	E4/5
Dubravkin put	D/E5
Frankopanska	D3
Gajeva	F1–3
Grgurova	E/F1
Grskovićeva	F5
Gundulićeva	E2/3
Hatza Pavla	F2
Haulikova	E1/2
Hebrangova	E2
Ilica	D/E3
Ilirski trg	E5
Jurišićeva	F3
Jurievska	E5
Kamenita	E4
Kaptol	F4
Katančićeva	F2
Klaićeva	D2
Koturaška	D/E1
Kovačićeva	D4/5, E2
Kršnjavoga	D2
Krležin Gvozd	D5
Krvavi most	E4
Kumičićeva	E1/2
Male stube	E4
Markov trg	E4
Masarykova	E3
Matičina	F2
Matoševa	E4
Medulićeva	D3
Medveščak	F5
Medvedgradska	F5
Mesnička	D3–E4
Mihanovićeva	D–F1
Mikloušićeva	F5
Miramarska cesta	E1
Miramarski podvožnjak	E1
Mletačka	E4
Nazorova	D4/5
Nova Ves	F4/5
Opatička	E4/5
Opatovina	F4
Paromlinska	F1
Perkovčeva	D2

Petrinjska	F1–3
Pod Zidom	F4
Praška	F3
Preradovićev trg	E3
Preradovićeva	E2/3
Prilaz Gjure Deželića	D3
Radićeva	E3/4
Ribnjak	F5
Runjaninova	D1/2
Savska	D2
Skalinska	F4
Starčevićev trg	F1
Streljačka	D4
Strossmayerovo šetalište	D/E4
Svačićev trg	E2
Teslina	F3
Tkalčićeva	E5–F4
Tomićeva	E3/4
Trg bana Josipa Jelačića	F3
Trg Brezov 29.X.1918	E4
Trg Dolac	F4
Tuškanac	D4/5
Unska	D1
Varšavska	E3
Visoka	D/E4
Vlaška	F3
Vodnikova	D1
Vrazova šetalište	E5
Vukotinovićeva	D2
Zamenhoffova	D5
Zvonarnička	F5
Ierjavićeva	E2

Dubrovnik

Antuninska	B2/3
Boškovićeva	B2/3
Bunićeva poljana	B2
C. Medovića	A2–B3
Ćubranovićeva	A2
Dordićeva	A/B2
Dropčeva	B2/3
Garište	A2
Getaldićeva	A2
Grada	B/C3
Gučetićeva	B2
Gundulićeva poljana	B2
Hvarska	C3
Ispod mira	C1
Izmedu polača	B2
Izmedu Vrta	A3
Kn. Damjana Jude	C2
Kovačka	B2–C3
Krešimira IV.	C3
Kunićeva	B2/3
Lučaria	B2
Luža	B/C2
N. Božidarevića	B2
Nalješkovićeva	B2/3
Od Domina	A2
Od Kaštela	A1/2
Od Margarite	A/B1
Od Puča	A/B2
Od Rupa	A2
Od Sigurate	B2/3
Palmotićeva	B2/3
Petilovrijenci	B2/3
Placa (Stradun)	A/B2
Poljana Marina Držića	C2
Poljana P. Miličevića	A2
Poljana R. Boškovića	B1
Ponta	C2
Porporelao	C2
Pred dvorom	C2
Prijeko	B3–C2
Put Iza	A/B3
Put Petra	B/C3
Ribarnica	C2
Strossmayerova	B2
·iroka	A/B2
Sv. Dominika	C2
Sv. Josipa	A/B2
Uska	B2
Uz posat	A3
Vetranićeva	B2/3
Vrta od Buže	B3
Za Rokom	A2
Zamanjina	B2/3
Zeljarica	B/C2
Zlatarićeva	A2
Zlatarska	C2/3
Iudioska	B2/3

Index

Index

Index

Picture Credits

Credits

1st Edition 2016

Worldwide Distribution: Marco Polo Travel Publishing Ltd
Pinewood, Chineham Business Park
Crockford Lane, Chineham
Basingstoke, Hampshire RG24 8AL, United Kingdom.
© MAIRDUMONT GmbH & Co. KG, Ostfildern

Authors: Tony Kelly, James Stewart, Daniela Schetar-Köthe
Editor: Frank Müller, Anja Schlatterer, Anette Vogt (red.sign, Stuttgart)
Revised editing and translation: Christopher Wynne
Program supervisor: Birgit Borowski
Chief editor: Rainer Eisenschmid

Cartography: © MAIRDUMONT GmbH & Co. KG, Ostfildern
3D-illustrations: jangled nerves, Stuttgart

Printed in China

Despite all of our authors' thorough research, errors can creep in.
The publishers do not accept any liability for this. Whether you
want to praise us, alert us to errors or give us a personal tip –
please don't hesitate to email or post to:

MARCO POLO Travel Publishing Ltd
Pinewood, Chineham Business Park
Crockford Lane, Chineham
Basingstoke, Hampshire RG24 8AL
United Kingdom
Email: sales@marcopolouk.com

FSC
www.fsc.org
MIX
Paper from
responsible sources
FSC® C020056

10 REASONS
TO COME BACK AGAIN

1. **Zagreb** has so many **museums** that can hardly all be visited on one trip.

2. There is so much to discover in **Istria's regional cuisine** in every season.

3. Croatian hospitality knows no bounds – you can never get enough of it!

4. There are always new beaches to explore on the Mediterranean's most **beautiful stretch of coastline**.

5. **Sublime sites** – tracing treasures from Antiquity in Croatia will keep you busy for a long time.

6. **Šnops** – schnaps, as a welcome drink – takes some getting used to, but helps break the ice.

7. **Island hopping** – more than 1100 islands, each with its own flair, are waiting to be explored.

8. **Addictive gourmet dining** – fresh fish from the Adriatic, sweet scampi and aromatic truffles.

9. Having been diving once, you will want to see more of the **fascinating undersea world**.

10. The flair from the days of imperial rule – every year, **magnificent, newly renovated buildings** open their doors.